Essentials of French Employment Law

Susan Hardie

Matador
9 Priory Business Park,
Wistow Road, Kibworth Beauchamp,
Leicestershire. LE8 0RX
Tel: 0116 279 2299
Email: books@troubador.co.uk
Web: www.troubador.co.uk/matador
Twitter: @matadorbooks

ISBN 978 178901 562 1

British Library Cataloguing in Publication Data.
A catalogue record for this book is available from the British Library.

Typeset in 10.5pt Aldine by Troubador Publishing Ltd, Leicester, UK

Matador is an imprint of Troubador Publishing Ltd

Contents

Contents

1. Introduction

French employment law is an extensive branch of law and it is not the purpose of this book to set out the whole of the law or the detail, but to set out the basics in a format that is comprehensible and accessible to English speakers. This book deals primarily with employment in the private sector, and not the public sector.

Substantial references are given for the relevant rules in the *Code du travail* or other laws/cases, to enable cross-checking and also research at source for more detail.

The French terms are used frequently (and always in italics) to introduce them for ease of comprehension of employment matters in practice in France/with French speakers. Where French terms appear for the first time in the text, a definition/explanation in English will be given. Wherever a French word appears in italics, it can also be looked up in the glossary at the end of the book to easily find the definition/explanation.

There is also an English–French glossary, which enables the French equivalent for English employment law terms to be found easily.

N.B. Recent reforms have sought to replace all the former employees' representative bodies such as the *CE* (*comité d'entreprise* – work's council) and the *CHSCT* (*comité d'hygiène, de sécurité et des conditions de travail* – committee for hygiene, safety and work conditions) with 1 sole body, the *CSE* (*comité social et économique* – social and economic committee). Other than where the Code is specifically dealing with the replacement of the bodies with the *CSE*, the Code now generally only refers to the *CSE*. Information relating to the previous bodies is therefore set out in an Appendix to this book, for reference purposes only.

There will be some circumstances where e.g. dismissals were already underway before recent reforms were published, and in those situations previous laws in effect at that time may apply. This book (other than the Appendix referred to above) will only deal with the new law as set out in the Code and not the previous law.

English law tends to approach whether there is a claim that can be made by an employee following a dismissal by considering possible wrongful dismissal (basically, a breach of contract) and unfair dismissal (which might for example be procedural or e.g. discriminatory), and that might involve looking at redundancy (where work positions are changing/reducing due to reduced business). Under French law the considerations, rules and principles are broadly similar but the initial approach is slightly different. There are specific procedures and principles for dismissals codified in detail in the *Code du travail* (the French employment law code) which vary depending largely upon whether the contract was fixed term or not (other factors may also be relevant). There is extremely limited scope for dismissal of employees on a fixed term contract. For other contracts, employees may be dismissed for reasons relating to the employee (e.g. certain disciplinary matters) or for economic reasons (which is like redundancy), but always complying with procedural rules and certain principles such as non-discrimination.

This book covers the essentials of French Employment Law (only). N.B. for legal advice in specific cases always consult the up to date complete legal sources and/or a lawyer.

2. French employment law

A) Legal professionals

In France the legal profession includes *huissiers* who deal with debt recovery and enforcement of judgements; *avocats* who carry out contentious work and advocacy, as well as company and commercial law, employment law etc; *notaires* who have a monopoly on some procedures relating to e.g. property transactions, and who deal with non-contentious matters including property work, company and commercial, tax, inheritance etc. There is therefore some overlap between the roles, however they are each entirely separate legal qualifications requiring different training. There is also a range of judicial roles which, when they involve a legal professional, each require their own separate training and qualification.

B) Sources of law

1) Law with national origins
a) Law created by the State
The French Constitution of 1958:
Created various economic and social rights, including the right to strike, freedom of unions, the right to work
  Laws and ordinances made by the French parliament setting the underlying principles for the rights and obligations applicable to all employees and employers
  Règlements and *décrets* relating to the application of laws.

b) Droit Conventionnel
Collective contracts and agreements made between unions of employees and of employers.

c) Contrat de Travail
Work contracts agreed between an employer and an employee setting out the terms and conditions of employment of the latter.

d) Usage professionnel
Unwritten rules (e.g. work customs and traditions/habitual arrangements) applicable in that area of work or in that particular business, which will usually tend to be incorporated into the relevant laws, conventions and collective agreements.

e) Jurisprudence
This does not mean the same as the English word jurisprudence, which relates more to the philosophy/theory behind the law.

The French word refers to the interpretation made by the courts or *tribunaux* of the texts of the laws and conventions during the course of court proceedings.

2) EU sources
a) EU *réglements*
The EU has created principles of freedom of movement for employees and the harmonisation of social legislation, which includes employment law.

b) Bilateral treaties
Treaties entered into between France and another country with mutual effect on a particular topic.

c) Conventions of the OIT
Recommendations of the International Employment Organisation (*Organisation International du Travail*) inviting the States that are party to it to make social reforms. These conventions only apply in a given country once that country has ratified it.

C) Hierarchy of sources of law

EU and International law
French Constitution
Laws and rules (*lois et réglements*)
Collective agreements (*conventions colléctives*)
Employment contract

D) Code du travail

The whole of French employment law is codified and gathered into 1 source, the *Code du travail*. This is made up of 3 parts (*parties*), each composed of nine books (*livres*).

- First part: legislation (*texts législatifs*) – indicated in references by an abbreviation to letter L

- Second part: rules (*réglements*) and decrees (*décrets*) from the *Conseil d'État* – indicated in references by an abbreviation to letter R

- Simple decrees (*décrets*) – indicated in references by an abbreviation to letter D.

Example of a reference: article L. 135–4

E) French courts

There are different courts depending upon the nature of the issue:

1) Civil jurisdictions
Courts of first instance
- the *tribunaux d'instance (T.I.)* court of first instance – 1 single judge (*juge*)

- *tribunaux de grande instance (T.G.I.)* – dealing with larger matters and with matters relating to land. Generally composed of at least 3 judges *(collégiale)*. The TGI has 3 specialised sections, the *chambre civile* (the civil court), the *chambre commerciale* (commercial court) and the *chambre correctionnelle* (the latter being the criminal section)

- *tribunaux de commerce* commercial courts – composed of non-professional judges (*juges consulaires*) being businessmen elected by their peers

- *Le conseil de prud'hommes* employment courts – composed of an equal number of representatives of employers and employees elected by their peers.

Court of Appeal
- *la Cour d'appel*

- *chambre d'accusation* section of the *Cour d'appel* dealing with appeals related to the jurisdictional aspects of criminal matters

- *chambre civile* civil section

- *chambre correctionnelle* criminal section

- *chambre sociale* dealing with so-called "social law" (*droit social* – particularly in relation to becoming unemployed, retiring, work holidays, incapacity etc. and often including employment issues generally).

La Cour de cassation

This is the final court of appeal. It is composed of 3 civil chambers, 1 commercial, economic and financial, 1 social and 1 criminal chamber. The composition of the court depends upon the nature of the action before it.

2) Criminal jurisdiction

The initial court section is the *juge d'instruction*, whose job is to gather together all the relevant information and evidence (*les preuves*) and to consider the charges (*les charges*) against the accused (*la personne mise en examen*) and to decide whether to transfer the matter to the judging sections of the court, depending on the gravity of the charges in question:

- *tribunal de police*

- *tribunal correctionnel*

- *la cour d'assises*

- *la Cour de cassation.*

3. Employment

French legislation does not provide a definition for a contract of employment.

The sources of law enabling a finding of a contract of employment are therefore largely to be found in case law, more particularly in rulings by the *Cour de cassation* on occasions where it has been necessary to assess whether a particular set of circumstances constitute a work contract.

The Court has held that the existence of a contract of employment does not depend either on the wish expressed by the parties or on the name that they have given to the arrangement but on the conditions as a matter of fact in which the activity of the workers is carried out: *"l'existence d'une relation de travail ne depend ni de la volonté exprimée par les parties ni de la denomination qu'elles ont donnée à leur convention mais des conditions de fait dans lesquelles est exercée l'activité des travailleurs"*.[1]

French law requires 3 conditions to be met for a situation of employment to exist to which employment law would apply:

- work provided to another

- remuneration of salary from that other

- a situation of legal subordination to that other.

A presumption that there is no employment applies to people registered as companies or at the register of businesses, on the register of commercial agents or with *Ursaff*.[2]

A presumption that there is a contract of employment exists for some other categories, for example for *VRP*s *(Voyageur, représentant et placier* – a French term for a particular class of salaried sales representatives)[3] journalists[4] and models.[5]

---

1   Cass. soc. 19 décembre 2000n *Dr. soc.,* 2001, p227. Cass. soc. 1er décembre 2005, *JCP S,* 2006, 1115. Cass. soc. 17 septembre 2008 *JCP S*, 2008, 1580. Cass. soc. 3 juin 2009, *JCP S,* 2009, Act. 305
2   art. 120-3 CW (loi 1994; abrogée en 1998, restauré par loi 2 août 2003)
3   art. L.7313-1 C. trav.
4   art. L.7112-1 C. trav.
5   art. L.7123-3 C. trav.

With regard to subordination, the Court held that the relationship of subordination is characterised by the execution of work under the authority of an employer who has the power to give orders and directives, to control the execution and to punish the failings of the employee – *"le lien de subordination est caracterisé par l'execution d'un travail sous l'autorité d'un employeur qui a le pouvoir de donner des orders et des directives, d'en controller l'execution et de sanctionner les manquements de son subordonné"*.[6]

A set of criteria (*faisceau d'indices*) rather than any specific criterion is generally used by the *Cour de Cassation*[7] to assist in determination as to whether subordination exists, looking at issues such as:

1. integration of the worker into an organised service:
*   whether the worker is required to comply with specific work hours

*   where the place of work is

*   whether the worker owns and uses his own work tools/equipment for his work.

2. the degree of power of control and penalty that the possible employer has. French employment law would apply to workers in the private sector and in public sector organisations having an industrial or commercial nature not subject to any particular law or laws governing such public bodies.

French employment law would not apply for example to unpaid people working for charity, or to *"professions libérales"* (specific professions requiring certain types of formal training and structure of employment, e.g. lawyers, doctors, architects).

---

6   Cass. soc. 13 novembre 1996 n *Dr. soc.,* 1996, p. 1067, note J.-J. Dupeyroux, *RJS*, 12/1996, n° 1320

7   Cass. Soc., 13 novembre 1996, Société Générale, Bull. Civ. V, n°386; Dr. Soc. 1996, p. 1067, note J.-J. Dupeyroux; JCP E 1997, Tome II, p.911, note Barthélémy; RJS 12/96, n° 1320; Grands arrêts, n° 2; Rép. Min. n° 7103, JO AN du 6 août 2013

4. Access to work

Broadly speaking, applications to work must comply with 3 criteria: they must be free, there must be equal treatment (non-discriminatory), and the offer of work must be transparent.

A) Bodies dealing with the search for and obtaining of work

1) Public employment service – *Service public d'emploi*

These bodies deal with seeking/finding work, payment, re-integration into the workforce, training and support for work seekers. There are 3 main categories:

a) **Those responsible for ensuring the provision of the service**: *Pôle emploi, l'Association nationale pour la formation professionnelle des adultes (AFPA)* and bodies dealing with *l'assurance chômage* (in this case, unemployment benefits).

b) **Public and private bodies which provide services** relating to the search for work, re-integration into the workforce, training and support for work-seekers, bodies related to the State by a *convention*, agencies dealing with temporary work, as well as private employment agencies.

c) **Bodies that participate or work with the public service**, e.g. public bodies that are separate from the State and have legal autonomy and own and manage their own resources and their divisions (*collectivités territoriales*).

When a job-seeker applies to one of the organisations, their file will be entered into a central information system to which all of the above would have access.

Local *communes* can enter into a *convention* with the State and the *Pôle* and are then entitled to receive details of job offers and undertake the services relating to the obtaining of work for the people falling within their administrative area.

Pôle emploi

The *Pôle emploi* is a national public body under the charge of the minister for employment, responsible for various matters relating to the work market:

- finding work offers and providing a database of them, and helping both employers in their search for employees and drawing offers to the attention of individuals in their search for work

- providing assistance to all persons seeking work, training or advice to assist in seeking a change of level of work/profession or promotion

- assisting all employers with employment and changes of level of their employees

- managing certain payments

- All people looking for work should register with the *Pôle emploi,* which should keep the database up to date.

Maisons de l'emploi

These are created in each region of France for bringing together the State, the *Pôle emploi collectivités territoriales* and, where applicable, consular bodies, *missions locales* (organisation set up to assist people aged 16 to 25 with regard to the search for work, with training and qualifications, housing and health matters, training bodies etc.

Their role is to:

- bring together the resources of the public service agencies relating to employment, to make the systems run more efficiently for employers and for job-seekers

- improve the national impact and effect of the services

- become involved in procedures relating to the re-classifying of levels of employees who have lost their employment or are threatened with a loss of employment.

Missions locales pour l'insertion professionnelle et sociale des jeunes Local agencies for assisting in the professional and social setting up of young people

These bodies were set up to assist people aged 16 to 25 to deal with all problems relating to entering the workforce and setting themselves up socially (i.e. mainly in relation to health and housing) and to provide information, advice, support and assistance.

2) Private employment services

This refers to those which provide a regular and habitual service seeking to bring together offers for and seekers of work, whilst not themselves becoming party to the employment relationship that may result.

Any physical or legal person (legal person in this case means a type of company, rather than a human or group of humans) intending to engage in this activity must first register with the administrative authority.

The provision of employment services referred to excludes all other activity intended to be for financial gain, with the exception of services providing recruitment advice, and advice relating to re-integration into the workforce.

No employment service may be refused to a person seeking work or to an employer for any discriminatory reason.

Services should be provided free to those seeking work; however, employers may be charged for assisting them in finding employees.

B) Offers of employment

Offers of employment may be freely circulated. The sale of offers of or notices of seeking work is not legal. Charges may be made for placing offers of or notices of seeking work in publications or other methods of communication.

Offers of work must not be discriminatory.[8] All offers published or otherwise circulated must be dated.

1) Recruitment

An employer should initially sort through the candidates, using criteria that should be set out for that particular post. This will be done by assessment of the CV of the applicant and any accompanying letter (*lettre de candidature*). The employer may then use various other selection methods, e.g. a probationary period, psychological tests, employment questionnaires, interviews etc.

Information requested may relate only to the applicant's capability to carry out that particular work and any professional or other work qualifications and or skills. There must be a clear and necessary link between the information sought and the work proposed or assessment of the related skills and qualifications.[9] The applicant must reply in good faith.[10]

8   art. L.1132-1 C. trav, art. 225-1 code pénal
9   art. L.1221-6 C. trav.
10   art. L.1221-6 C. trav.

Where the business has 50 or more employees, the information received from the applicant in writing must be assessed under conditions of anonymity by the employer. The *Conseil d'État* provides prescribed systems for carrying this out.

2) Obtaining work

Minimum age

The minimum age for seeking work is 16 years,[11] which is the end of the obligatory period of education under French law. Holiday work may be started at the age of 14 years;[12] apprenticeships and similar specific types of work placements specifically to lead to particular types of qualification may be started at the age of 15 years.[13]

There are various restrictions on the work that may be carried out by *jeunes travailleurs* (young workers – i.e. those under 18 including trainees/people on work experience)[14] with a view to protecting them. For example, children older than 14 years may for up to half of their school holidays carry out light work.[15] The employer should obtain the prior permission of the *inspecteur du travail* (work inspector employed by the State). As another example, the *inspecteur* may at any moment require a medical examination of a young worker of 15 years or more to check that the work they are doing does not exceed their capacity.[16]

Non-discrimination[17]

There are comprehensive anti-discrimination rules.

No person may be prejudiced with regard to a recruitment procedure, any type of apprenticeship or training in a company; no employee may be subject to any disciplinary penalty, dismissed or made the subject of any discriminatory action, particularly with regard to remuneration, training, *reclassement* (*classification* refers to the process of classifying an employee in respect of their level or category of work) of level, of assignment, of qualification, of *classification*, of promotion, of geographical relocation or of renewal of contract by reason of:

- origin, sex, beliefs, sexual orientation, age, family situation, genetic characteristics, belonging either in fact or allegedly to an ethnic group, a nation or a race, political opinions, union activities or social movement,

---

11   art. L.4153-1 C. trav.
12   art. L.4153-1, art. L.4153-2 C. trav.
13   art. L.4153-1 C. trav.
14   art. L.3161 C. trav.
15   art. L.4153-3 C. trav.
16   art. L.4153-4 C. trav.
17   art. L.1132-1 C. trav. art. 225 code penal. Other articles in the C. trav. supplement the requirements

religious convictions, physical appearance, family name or (other than with regard to an incapacity to do the work certified by the work doctor) by reason of health or disability

- having been subjected to or refused sexual harassment, or having witnessed or disclosed sexual harassment.

Priorities to offer work to certain types/groups of potential employee
As a preliminary step to filling an employment role, and before more generally seeking a person to fill it, an employer must ensure that there are no employees who are entitled to a priority of employment.

Different categories of priority exist, for example:

- priority to be offered the post, relevant employees currently in a part-time employment there[18]

- the right for an employee to be re-integrated at the end of maternity leave or a leave for "parental education" (which is a specific type of leave available to parents in France),[19] sick leave or leave for an accident/injury at work, a study leave or a sabbatical

- priority to be re-employed (this priority lasts for 1 year) for an employee whose contract was ended or who could not be re-employed (dismissal for economic reasons[20] or postnatal leave)

- obligation to employ disabled people; in general (and subject to various regulations on the practical application of the rule) all employers must fill 6% of the posts with disabled people.[21] This obligation can for example be adjusted at least in part by making a payment or provision of other specified benefits.[22]

Employment of foreigners
As a basic principle, nationals from an EU member country may be employed anywhere in the EU.[23] There remain limits in respect of persons from some countries. The receiving country may require a document of

---

18 art. L.3123-3 C. trav.
19 art. L.1225-67 C. trav.
20 art. L.1233-45 C. trav.
21 arts. L.5212-2 C. trav.
22 e.g. arts. L.5212-6 and L. 5212-9 C. trav.
23 Consolidated version of the Treaty on the Functioning of the European Union – PART THREE: UNION POLICIES AND INTERNAL ACTIONS – TITLE IV: FREE MOVEMENT OF PERSONS, SERVICES AND CAPITAL – Chapter 1: Workers – Article 45 (ex Article 39 TEC)

proof of right to residence, e.g. a passport from an EU member country.

Nationals from non-EU countries must comply with the requirements administered by *l'Agence national de l'accueil des étrangers et des migrations* (*ANAEM*). To carry out an activity, the non-EU worker must obtain a permit, which authorises the right to reside and the right to work (this will either be a *carte de séjour temporaire* or a *carte de résident*, which would be valid for 10 years).

C) Formalities of the act of employing

1) Registers

There are a number of registers that a potential employer may be required to keep such as:

le régistre unique du personnel
le régistre des délégués du personnel
le régistre des contrôles techniques de sécurité
le régistre des accidents du travail bénins
le régistre des mises en demeure
le régistre du CSE (this can be kept as a joint register with the *régistre des mises en demeure*).

2) Notices

There are also mandatory notices that should be put up in a work place such as:

l'inspection du travail: nom, adresse, téléphone
le service médical du travail: adresse, téléphone
texts dealing with professional and remuneration equality between the sexes
where there are more than 50 employees, notices relating to safety and fire
le document unique d'évaluation des risques professionnels[24] – a document setting out the health and safety risks of the workplace/work and the measures in place to address them
notification of the existence of *un accord de participation*
union notices
the communal working hours.

---

24   arts. L.4121-1 à 3 et R.4121-1 et 2 C. trav.

Other documents must also be distributed in an appropriate manner including:

interior rules

notifications of the existence of *conventions collectifs* and/or *accords collectifs d'entreprise*

days and hours of general non-working entitlement where all the employees do not have an entitlement to weekly rest for the whole of Sunday

copy of the information submitted to the *inspection du travail* in the event of a suspension of weekly time off where legally required

documents setting out the rules and procedures on sexual harassment and workplace bullying

documents setting out the rules and procedures dealing with discrimination in employment applications

list of the members of the *CSE*

the order of the dates for the start of holidays.

3) Declarations

Prior to employing a person the employer must make a declaration to the social protection agency covering their area (this might be the *Ursaff* – social security authority, or for agricultural employees the body is known as the *caisse de mutualité agricole* – agricultural mutual),[25] no later than the last day prior to employing the person (*déclaration d'embauche*). The agency will provide to the employer a document confirming reception of the declaration.

The declaration shall include at least the following information:

- the name of the business (registered where applicable), *code APE* (*Activité Principale Exercée*: this will be the code for the principal activity from a set list of codes) and address of the employing business

- the family name, first names, nationality, date and place of birth, social security number, date and time of commencement of employment.

4) Rules regarding the creation of a contract

The creation of a contract must comply with certain basic rules:[26]

- the consent of the parties to enter into the contract must be free, mutual and not a result of any type of mistake, violence or fraud

---

25 art. L.1221-10 C. trav.
26 art. L.1221-1 C. trav.

- the parties must have the legal capacity to enter into the contract

- the aim of the contract must be legal, possible and either certain or capable of being determined

- the reason for the contract must not be contrary to public order or immoral.

The employer is deemed to undertake to:

- provide the work and the means to do it

- pay the employee the sums due when due

- comply with all applicable laws, rules, collective agreements etc.

- pay all relevant mandatory contributions (e.g. social security payments, unemployment insurance)

The employee is deemed to undertake to:

- carry out the work personally and conscientiously

- take due care of tools, equipment, materials etc. provided for the work

- comply with the internal rules of the organisation

- not disclose trade secrets (*secret professionel*) or enter into competition (*concurrence*).

5) Contractual document rules

As a general principle, the contract itself does not usually have to be in writing, and can take any form that the contracting parties decide to adopt.[27] Normally any offer of employment does not have to comply with a particular form either. However certain types of contract do have particular requirements. A *contrat de travail à durée déterminée* (fixed term contract), *contrat de travail temporaire* (temporary work contract) and *contrat de travail à temps partiel* (part-time work contract) should be in writing setting out certain obligatory points.

A document showing the following must however be created showing the essential conditions of the work contract (in compliance not least with the European directive of 14 October 1991):

---

27   art. L.1221-1 II C. trav.

- the place of work

- a description of the work

- the salary

- the length of the employment

- the holiday/other entitlement to time off work.

At the commencement of the employment the employer must give to the employee a document setting out the information contained in the *déclaration unique d'embauche (DUE)*.

As soon as it is received the employer must also give to the employee the detachable section of the document from the agency confirming receipt of the declaration. This receipt will again set out the details included in the declaration. If the contract of employment is completed at the point of commencement of the employment with the details of the identity of the agency, the employer does not have to provide the detachable section to the employee.

6) External notifications following completion of the contract

The employer must enter the new employee in the register of employees (*régistre unique de personnel*), which is a mandatory document. It may be kept on a computer (i.e. not in hard copy).

If the employee has never been registered with the *Sécurité sociale* (the State body in France which handles family, health and retirement benefits and litigation arising) then it is the obligation of the employer to have the employee registered within eight days following the commencement of the employment.

The employer must arrange a medical assessment of the new employee (*la visite médicale d'embauche*). The assessment must take place no later than before the expiry of any trial period of the employee.

For all enterprises with at least 50 employees, during the first 8 days of each month the employer must deliver to the *DDTE* (*Direction Départementale du Travail et de l'Emploi* – Department of Labour and Employment) a summary of the employment contracts entered into or ended.

7) Modifications to the contract

The employee may request these, however the employer is only obliged to agree in certain limited circumstances, e.g. a request by a pregnant employee who seeks an alternative form of work due to their health, or a parent seeking part-time work to look after their children.

The employer may alter the contract for valid reasons relating to the competence of the employee or for economic reasons. They may also alter the conditions of work, e.g. the office hours. If the change is for a reason relating to the employee themselves or only relates to the work conditions, then the employee is obliged to accept the change or hand their notice in (following applicable procedures). If however the motive is economic, the employee is not obliged to accept the change. If they do not, then the employer may either renounce the modification or dismiss the employee (following applicable procedures).

Where the form or ownership of the employer changes, the contract will usually transfer unchanged to the new structure.

D) Distance working

The situations in which employees may be entitled to work from home have been extended. Currently this right will usually be dependent on an *accord collectif* or if none, an arrangement set up by the employer after obtaining the advice of the *comité social and économique*. If an employer wishes to oppose distance working for an eligible employee, they must provide a reason/reasons.[28]

E) Illegal work – *Travail Dissimulé (Clandestin)*

This is a serious criminal offence for which fines of up to 45,000 euros or even prison sentences of up to 3 years may be imposed.[29] A civil penalty of 6 months' salary may also be payable.[30]

The offence may include[31] any case where there is any part of or whole of the production, of transformation or of the provision of services for profit by any person whether physical or in the sense of a corporate person or similar (a company may be said to have *moral* or a legal personality, so that it is treated legally much as a physical person would be in the sense that for example it can take or defend legal proceedings) where there is a failure to carry out the following obligations:

- registration of the business where obligatory on the *répertoire des métiers* (a register of non-incorporated businesses) or the *régistre du commerce des sociétés* (register of companies)

---

28   art. L.1222-9 C.trav.
29   art. L.8224-1 C. trav.
30   art. L.8223-1 C. trav.
31   art. L.8211 C. trav.

- mandatory declarations to the agencies for social protection and fiscal authorities

- carry out at least 2 of the following obligations with respect to employees: provision of pay slips, keeping a *livre de paie* (register of salaries, bonuses etc.) or the *régistre unique de personnel* (register of personnel).

The offence is also committed if a business seeks to inappropriately sub-contract in conditions such that the requirements for an employment contract are fulfilled.

5. Contract

A contract exists where a work activity is carried out under the authority of an employer. Whilst the contract may be in any form agreed by the parties[32] and may also contain terms and conditions agreed freely between the parties, subject to legal and conventional rules, various recognised types of contract exist.

The terms of a contract may be agreed directly between the parties.

They may also be created or overwritten by an *accord*.[33] Previously various types of *accords d'entreprises* (e.g. for reduction in work time, mobility etc.) applied to the work contract and if employees refused them they could be dismissed. Now there will be 1 type of *accord* that will be used to cover contract terms, but it will cover a wider field (good running of the enterprise, development or preservation of employment). Employees who refuse the changes will be dismissed for "specific reasons" (*motif spécifique*) which constitute *cause réelle et sérieuse*.[34]

The subjects for negotiation will be divided into 3 different groups for the purposes of assessing hierarchies of precedence:[35]

* where the *accord de branche* (agreement between 1 or more employers and 1 or more representatives of the employees (unions) in a given sector of work) will take precedence: conventional minima, classification of roles, mutualisation of financial benefits such as *prévoyance* and training, management and quality of the work (part-time, short contracts etc.), professional equality

* where the professional or work sector may decide if their *accords* take precedence over the *accords d'entreprise*: disciplinary rules, disability, conditions under which a union mandate may be exercised, bonuses for dangerous work

* the *accord d'entreprise* will take precedence for all the other matters, such as salary increases based on length of employment, the thirteenth-month salary.

---

32   art. L.1221-1 C. trav.
33   art. L.2254 C. trav.
34   art. L.2254 C. trav.
35   art. L.2253 C. trav.

There is a limited period during which it may be possible for pre-existing arrangements that breach the new norms to be ratified.

Currently a majority vote (*accord majoritaire*) is required mainly for decisions relating to the working hours. For other matters, the signature of minority unions representing 30% of the employees is sufficient, provided that the unions representing the majorities do not object.

From 1 May 2018 it is intended that the *accord majoritaire* will be the standard for all matters.[36]

A) General

The *Cour de cassation* has stated that "the existence of a work relationship depends neither upon the wish expressed by the parties nor the name that they have given to their agreement but on the conditions of fact in which the workers exercise their activity".[37]

A work contract is one under which a person (*le salarié*) undertakes to work for and under the direction of another person (*l'employeur*) and receives in return remuneration (*le salaire*).

Generally, the person seeking to prove the existence of a contract has the burden of proof.[38] In certain circumstances, such as where a person is registered in the French companies register, French law sets out a presumption of an absence of a contract of employment.[39] This presumption can be overturned.[40]

The limitation period for starting proceedings about the execution of a contract will usually be 2 years from the day that the claimant knew or ought to have known the facts that enabled them to bring the claim. The limitation period for claims about the ending of the contract is usually 12 months from the date of notification of the termination. There are variations that may apply in specific circumstances, e.g. where physical injury has occurred, or there has been discrimination.[41]

B) Two main types of contract

There are 2 main types of employment contract recognised under French law, each of which have their own applicable rules:

---

36 *Décret n° 2017-1398 of 25 September 2017
37 Cass. soc. 19 décembre 2000, Dr. soc., 2001, p.227. Cass. soc. 1er décembre. 2005n *JCP S* 2006, 115. Cass. soc. 17 septembre 2008. Cass. soc. juin 2009.
38 art. L.1221-1 C. trav.
39 L'alinéa 1er art. L.8221-6 C. trav.
40 L'alinéa 2, art. L.8221-6 C. trav.
41 art. L.1471-1 C. trav.

le contrat de travail à durée indéterminée (CDI) – contract with no fixed termination date; this is the more usual form of contract and is deemed to exist when no fixed term is agreed (i.e. unless otherwise arranged).[42] Thus it may be referred to as a *contrat de travail de droit commun* – common law form of contract. The employer and the employee each have the right to terminate it at any point (subject to applicable laws etc.)

le contrat de travail à durée déterminée (CDD) – fixed term contract; this will have a fixed end date or point. In general, its complete term must be carried out.

Broadly speaking, various specific types of contract exist. Sometimes the *CDI* will be used for that type and sometimes the *CDD*. However some types of contract may use either. Examples of these uses are as follows:

Les contrats de travail précaires – CDDs and temporary contracts:

le contrat de travail à durée déterminée	CDD
le contrat de travail temporaire d'intérim) – temporary work contract	CDD/CDI
le contrat de travail à temps partagé – job-share contract	CDI
le contrat de travail saisonnier – seasonal work contract	CDD
le contrat de chantier ou d'opération – contract for a project or job of work – previously mainly for construction industry but now for general use as well	CDI
le contrat de mission à l'exportation – contract for a project as expatriate	CDI
le CDD senior – fixed term contract for older employees	CDD
le CDD à objet défini – fixed term contract for a specific task	CDD
le contrat étudiant au sein des établissements d'enseignement supérieur – student contract based in a higher education establishment	CDD

Les contrats de travail destinés à l'aménagement du temps de travail – contracts intended to assist in organisation of work time:

le contrat de travail à temps partiel – part-time contract	CDD/CDI
le contrat de travail intermittent – contract for intermittent work	CDI

---

42   art. L.1221-2 C. trav.

Les contrats de travail destinés à la formation et/ou à l'insertion – **contracts for the purpose of work training/development or re-integration in employment:**

le contrat d'apprentissage – apprenticeship contract	*CDD/CDI*
le contrat de professionnalisation – type of contract combining work and work training	*CDD/CDI*
le contrat initiative-emploi (CIE) (also *le contrat d'accompagnement dans l'emploi - CA*) – contract where a subsidy is provided to the employer for the job, generally to enable those who are having difficulties finding employment for either social reasons or reasons relating to the area of work – usually retail sector	*CDD/CDI*
le contrat d'avenir (CAE) – type of contract particularly aimed at helping young people having various types of difficulty obtaining work, involving subsidy to the employer and additional support for the employee by e.g. tutors in the business and assistance from State bodies	*CDD/CDI*

New laws are intended to provide that an *accord de branche* may modify the length and/or number of renewals and period of delay in between *CDDs*.

They may also authorise use of a *CDI de chantier ou d'opération* contract for a project or job that can end once the particular work project has been completed, and which was previously mainly used in the construction industry but may now be used more generally.

6. Contract with no fixed term – *Contrat de travail à durée indéterminée (CDI)*

This is the general type of contract implied under French law. It may be part time or full time but it will not have an agreed end date or event.

(N.B. A certain type of contract is coming into existence known as a *contrat de projet*. This may technically be a *CDI* and is likely to be an extension of the *CDI de chantier,* which is a type of contract used for the purposes of a fixed piece of work but for which the time necessary is not certain. This type of contract will not usually lead to an entitlement to the *prime de précarité* at its end, being used specifically to enable employers to make contracts that have an ending at the conclusion of the particular project.)

A) Common clauses

Article L.1121-1 of the *Code du travail* limits clauses in that they must not restrict people and individual liberties in ways that are not justified by the nature of the task to be completed or are not proportionate (the principle of *proportionalité*) to the intended outcome.

1) Object clause – *Clause d'objectifs*
This must be reasonable and realistic, and the employee should be suitably qualified to perform the object but also the employer should provide the necessary facilities. Consequently failing to comply with/achieve the object will not automatically constitute a reason for dismissal. In assessing the reason for failing to comply with or achieve the object, the court should look at whether the employer has complied with the obligation to ensure that the employee is suitably qualified and has provided the necessary facilities, to check if the non-respect is in fact due to a fault by the employee.[43]

2) Trial period – *Périod d'essai*
There is no presumption of a trial period. To exist it must be stipulated expressly in the letter of engagement (*lettre d'embauche*) or contract.[44]

---

43   Cass. soc. 14 novembre 2000, Dr. Soc., 2001, p. 99
44   art. L.1221-23 C. trav.

There are legal maximum durations for a *période d'essai* set out in the *Code du travail*. In the case of a *CDI*, the maximum period depends upon the qualification classification of the work of the employee,[45] however shorter periods may be agreed in a collective agreement or in the contract of employment. The terms set out in the Code will be substituted for any that are shorter, renewals included, agreed in an *accord de branche* concluded before 25 June 2008.

There are provisions for renewal, once only, of the trial period, but only where an *accord de branche* provides for renewal, and where the contract or letter of engagement expressly provides for renewal.

Category of employee	Initial maximum duration	Total maximum duration including any renewal[46]
Ouvriers et employés	2 months	4 months
Agents de maitrise et techniciens	3 months	6 months
Cadres	4 months	8 months

Where a trial period applies, the usual provisions relating to the termination of the contract do not apply.[47] The contract may be terminated by either party during the period without providing a reason or any compensation (subject where applicable to paid leave entitlement or specific contractual provision to the contrary), but subject to respecting a notification period (*délai de prévenance*), the length of which will be between 24 hours and 1 month, depending upon the length of time the employee has been in the company.

Where the termination is at the instigation of the employer:[48]
8 days employment – 24 hours
Between 8 days and 1 month – 48 hours
Between 1 and 3 months – 2 weeks
Over 3 months – 1 month.

Where the termination is at the instigation of the employee:[49]
Less than 8 days employment – 24 hours
8 days or more – 48 hours.

---

45 art. L.1221-19 C. trav.
46 art. L.1221-21 C. trav.
47 art. L.1231-1 C. trav.
48 art. L.1221-25 C. trav.
49 art. L.1221-26 C. trav.

The courts have extended certain protections:

The termination must not be discriminatory[50] or abusive otherwise damages and interest (*dommages-intérêts*) may be awarded to the injured party (*partie lesée*).

Where the employer seeks to terminate the contract during the renewal period of a protected employee, then the works inspector (*inspecteur du travail*) must be notified in advance.[51]

The *période d'essai* is not the same as either *l'essai professionnel* or the *période probatoire*.

L'essai professionnel is a form of professional assessment carried out prior to any contract being entered into. Consequently salary will not apply but for example expenses may be paid.

La période probatoire applies where a current employee enters a trial period to assess them for a new position within the organisation. Terminating such a period does not terminate the contract but replaces the employee in their former role.

The employer must not take into account the pregnancy of an employee when considering terminating during a *période d'essai* but the existence of the pregnancy does not of itself prevent a termination during the *période d'essai*.[52]

An employee becoming unable to work by virtue of illness or injury, particularly where the cause is to do with the work, will have protection. As a general rule an employer is not allowed to terminate the employment of a person made unable to work by virtue of an accident at work or work-related illness unless there is *faute grave* by the employee or an impossibility to maintain the contract for reasons not related to the work-related illness/injury.[53]

3) Guarantee of employment clause – *Clause de garantie d'emploi*

Under such a clause, the employer guarantees not to terminate the employee's employment during a certain period (except by mutual agreement) otherwise damages and interest would become due. These would be calculated as the remuneration that the employee would have received had the period of guarantee been respected.[54] Furthermore, the employee still retains the right to claim, where applicable, *l'indemnité de licenciement* and *l'indemnité compensatrice de préavis*. They are not cumulated with *allocations chômage*.[55] Such a clause may provide for certain eventualities for which termination may nevertheless be allowed, e.g. economic reasons, fault, inaptitude of the employee for the task.

---

50   art. L.1132 C. trav.
51   Cass. soc., 26 octobre 2006, *RJS*, 2006, n° 63
52   art. L.1225-1 C. trav.
53   art. L.1226-9 C.trav.
54   Cass. soc. 27 octobre 1998, *D.*, 1999, JP, p. 186
55   Ass. plén. C. cass 13 décembre 2002, n° 00-17.143

4) Exclusivity – *Exclusivité*

This type of clause requires the employee not to carry out another work activity during the time of their employment. It must be indispensable to the protection of the legitimate interests of the enterprise, justified by the nature of the task and proportionate to the aim sought.[56] Such clauses are not valid against a part-time employee.[57] They may also not be used against an employee who takes or creates a business, for a period of 1 year following the end of their employment (although the employee retains a duty of loyalty to the employer).[58] This rule does not apply to certain types of worker, e.g. those whose job is to find buyers or markets for the company's produce. Breach of such a clause by an employee may constitute a *faute grave* which could lead to dismissal.

5) Non-competition – *Non-concurrence*

This clause would prevent the employee from setting up in work in competition with the employer following the end of their employment (which could also be after an employee has carried out a *période d'essai*). To apply, it should be provided for in the work contract or *convention collective*. In the second case it must also be notified to the employee, but does not have to also be in the contract.

Such a clause should comply with the relevant provisions of the *Code du travail*.[59] It will be *nulle* (void) unless it complies with all of the following.

It must:

- be necessary to the protection of the legitimate interests of the enterprise

- be limited in time

- be limited in place

- take account of the particularities of the employment of that employee: the employee should be left in a position where they can nevertheless use their training, qualifications and experience elsewhere

- provide a pecuniary recompense (*contrepartie pécuniaire*) for the employee. The calculation of this may be fixed by the *convention collective*, however if it has not been then the parties are free to agree the amount subject to a basic requirement that it shall not be derisory.[60] The sum would be due upon the

---

56 art. L.1121-1 C. trav.
57 Cass. soc., 11 juill. 2000, n° 98-43.240, JSL 3 oct. 2000, n° 65-2
58 art. L.1222-5 C. trav.
59 art. L.1221-1 C.trav.
60 Cass. soc. 15 novembre 2006, Dr. soc., 2007, p. 241

actual departure of the employee from the business, and not the theoretical expiration of the notice period. If the payment is not made, the employee is no longer bound by the *clause de non-concurrence*, and may nevertheless claim the payment plus damages and interest which is intended to cover the prejudice (that is to say, loss, inconvenience etc.) caused by the failure of the employer to comply with their obligation to pay.

Where the clause does not comply with the conditions, the employee also has a claim to annul the clause, and may claim damages and interest, which will be assessed by the court taking into account prejudice suffered by virtue of the failure of the employer to comply with their obligation. The judge may also reduce the amplitude of the clause with regard to time, space or other practicalities, by the degree to which they assess it to be excessive.

If the clause is inherently illegal then the employee need not comply with it, or may choose instead to claim damages and interest.[61]

If the employee breaches such a clause, the employer may claim damages and interest.

Since the clause relates to the post-employment period, only facts during that time may constitute a breach of the clause.[62]

If provided for in the contract or in the *convention collective*, or failing these with the consent of the employee, the employer may choose to renounce the clause (in a manner that is express and precise and results from a clear and unequivocal consent). The employee will then no longer be bound by it. In the event of a dispute in this case the onus would be on the employer to show that they had released the employee from the non-competition clause, if the employer wishes also to be released from the obligation to pay the *contrepartie pécuniaire*.

A prospective employer should check that prospective employees are free from such restrictions.

6) Clause for reimbursement of training costs – *Clause de dédit-formation*

This type of clause would provide that where an employee who has been provided with a training course then leaves, they must reimburse either the costs of the training or pay a penalty. Such a clause will only be valid if signed by the employee before the commencement of the training. The clause must also set out the cost of the training, any sums for which the employee will be responsible, and the date, nature and duration of the training.[63] The payment should relate to the costs incurred that are in excess of the minima required by law or by the *convention collective* and be proportional to the costs incurred by the training. It should not have the effect of depriving the employee of

---

61 Cass. soc. 11 janvier 2006, *Dr. soc.*, 2006, p. 456 ; JCP S, 2006, 1102
62 Cass. soc. 30 octobre 2007, n° 06-44.551
63 Cass. soc. 4 février 2004, *D.*, 2004, JP, p. 677

the ability to leave the job.[64] Such clauses will not usually be valid if used in contracts which are of a nature that is intended to integrate or re-integrate an employee into the workforce, for example with *jeunes salaries*.[65] They should also not be used in a *contrat de professionnalisation*.

7) Geographical mobility clause – *Clause de mobilité géographique*
This is a clause to entitle the employer to make any geographical changes to the place of employment. Even in the absence of such a clause, the employer may generally still change the place of employment if it remains within the same geographical sector and the employer provides sufficient notice.[66]

There is a great deal of case law ensuring the reasonable use of this power by employers. Any clause in the contract requiring geographical mobility must be clear, and must set out the applicable geographical areas.[67] The clause must be used with respect to the right to a personal and family life of the employee (pursuant to art. L.1121-1 of the *Code du travail*) and consequently any impact on this right must be justified by the task to be accomplished and proportionate to the aim sought.[68]

Where the employer is entitled to require a change of workplace, the employee may be in breach of contract for refusing to move and may risk dismissal.

B) Dismissal for reasons related to the individual – *Licenciement pour motif personnel*

1) Real and serious cause – *Une cause réelle et sérieuse*
The Code requires a real and serious cause[69] but does not define this; it is up to the judge to assess.

"Serious" implies that the situation makes the continuation of the work relationship impossible. This is not the same as "*faute grave*": there may be no "fault",[70] but the effect is such that the work relationship cannot continue.

The dismissal must relate to a cause that objectively rests on facts attributable to the individual concerned.[71]

There   are   various   disciplinary   justifications: insubordination,

---

64   Cass. soc. 21 mai 2002, *Dr. soc.*, 2002, p. 902
65   la loi du 31 décembre 1991 relative à la formation professionnelle; la loi du 4 mai 2004
66   Cass. soc, 30 mai 2013, n°12-16949
67   Cass. soc. 24 janvier 2008, *JCP S*, 2008 1250
68   Cass. soc. 14 octobre 2008, *JCP S*, 2008, 1668. Cass. soc. 13 janvier 2009, *Dr. soc.,* 2009, p. 611
69   art. L.1232-1 C. trav.
70   Soc. 25 avr. 1985 : Bull. civ. V, n°261 ; D. 1985. IR 381
71   Soc. 7 déc. 1993: D. 1994. Somm. 309, obs. A. Lyon-Caen et Papadimitrou

inappropriate receattitudes, breaches of trust or loyalty, violent behaviour, unjustified absences or having abandoned the post.

There are also various justifications that are not classified in themselves as disciplinary. These might include for example a failure to produce the right results.[72] This is not the same as professional insufficiency (*insuffisance professionnelle*) or inaptitude (*inaptitude professionnelle*). In either case, the employer must produce evidence of the facts that are the cause for concern, and the objectives must be realistic, reasonable and compatible with the market.[73]

Dismissal due to the health of the employee is not allowable unless there is prolonged or repeated absence of a nature that disrupts the functioning of the enterprise and makes it necessary to replace the employee definitively. Once the physical inability of the employee has been confirmed medically, the employer must first seek to reclassify the employee in the enterprise and only if this is impossible would dismissal be allowed.

Certain reasons may not be used for dismissal. This would include discriminatory reasons[74] or dismissal related to the normal exercise of the right to strike,[75] or *harcèlement moral*,[76] or *sexuel,* or where it relates to certain categories of employees, e.g. a pregnant woman, a protected employee, a victim of an accident at work or a work-related illness during the period of suspension of the work contract.

The exercise of freedom of expression, religious freedom, choice of home and the right to dress oneself are all matters which may not be used as a reason for a dismissal.[77]

a) Procedure

A letter calling the employee to a meeting must be sent by post *recommandé avec accusé de réception* or personally handed over and signed for.[78] The letter should fix a date for the meeting, which must be not less than 5 working days after the delivery of the letter. The employee is entitled to have 1 of the other employees with them at the meeting, which would be from the representation bodies, or if none then freely chosen from the employees, or by an employee adviser from the list prepared by the administrative authority. The letter of convocation should state that the employee may be accompanied by an external employee advisor from the list prepared by the administrative authority.[79]

The employee may request that the meeting is postponed to another date;

---

72   Soc. 3 févr. 1999, n° 97-40.606 P: D.1999. IR 6; JPC 1999 II. 10132, obs. Serret
73   Cass. soc.13 mars 2001, *Bull. civ.V,* n° 86, Cass. soc. 2 décembre 2003, RJS, 02/2004, n° 184
74   art. L.1132-1 C. trav.
75   art. L.1132-2 C. trav.
76   art. L.1152-3 et L.1153-4 C. trav.
77   Cass. soc. 28 avril 1988, *Dr. soc.,* 1988, p.428 (affaire Clavaud)
78   art. L.1232-2 C. trav.
79   art. L.1232-4 C. trav.

in that case a fresh letter must be sent complying with the same requirements for the postponement to be valid.

The employer must in the meeting set out to the employee the precise reasons for the meeting and possible dismissal. The employer must receive any explanation given by the employee.[80]

If the employer decides to proceed with the dismissal they must notify the employee of the decision by a letter sent *recommandé avec accusé de réception* which must be posted no less than 2 working days after the meeting. The letter must set out the exact reasons for the dismissal. A set form of letter is now to be used for this.[81] Recent reforms allow the employer within (currently) 15 days following the notification of the dismissal to detail the reasons that were set out in that letter.[82]

The date of the letter is the starting point for the notice period and enables the calculation of the length of service of the employee for the calculation of any sums due.

b) Notice – *Le préavis de licenciement*

Minimum notice periods apply depending upon the length of employment of the employee. The employee will usually be expected to work the notice period. Notice periods may be set by the Code or other laws, *convention collective*, *accord collectif*, the employment contract or the customs of the profession; the longest notice period will be the one that applies and it should not usually be shorter than, nor should the conditions of required length of employment in the enterprise usually be longer than, those set in the Code.[83]

There are adaptations to the usual rules that will apply, including where there has been *faute grave* or there is *inaptitude*.

The notice must be sent at least 2 *jours ouvrable* after the date of the *convocation* to an *entretien préalable* and specified model forms of letter should be used that will be set by *décret*[84] (see above under Procedure).

Where the dismissal is for *inaptitude médicale*, having followed the appropriate other procedure in such cases, the notice itself may not be worked but where the *inaptitude* is related to the work then an indemnity will be due to the employee.[85]

Contents of the notice

Specified model forms of letter should be used that will be set by *décret*.[86]

---

80   art. L.1232-3 C. trav.
81   art. L.1232-6 C. trav.
82   art. L.1253-2 C. trav.
83   E.g. art. L.1234-2 C. trav.
84   art. L.1232-6 C. trav.
85   art. L.1226-4 C. trav.
86   art. L.1232-6 C. trav.

The letter of notice must set out the ground(s) for the dismissal.[87] Failure to comply will be a procedural error but will no longer automatically lead in court proceedings to an assessment of the actual legal basis for the dismissal. Recent reforms allow the employer within 15 days following the notification of the dismissal to detail reasons that were set out in that letter.

The letter should not simply be a referral to the grounds as set out in the *convocation* calling the employee to the *entretien préalable*.

There may be any number of personal reasons but not a mixture of personal reasons and economic ones.

The usual minimum notice periods are:[88]

Less than 6 months	Notice period depends upon the law, *convention* or *accord collectif* or in default, the customs in the area and the profession
Between 6 months and 2 years	Minimum 1 month
At least 2 years	Minimum 2 months

Effect of the letter of notice

The notice does not start to run until the date that the letter is presented to the employee.[89]

The letter also sets the limitation dates for court proceedings.[90]

c) Compensation – *Indemnité de licenciement*

Compensation will be payable to employees who have worked for that employer for 8 months who are dismissed, with exceptions such as in cases of *faute grave*.[91]

The compensation should not be less than a quarter of a month's salary per year of employment up to 10 years of employment, and a third of a month's salary will be added per year over 10 years of employment.[92]

The compensation will be calculated either on the basis of 1) the monthly average of the remuneration received by the employee in the last 12 months preceding the dismissal or if less than 12 months, the monthly average for the whole of those months or 2) on the basis of one third of the salaries received

---

87   art. L.1232-6 C. trav.
88   art. L.1234-1 C. trav.
89   art. L.1234-3 C. trav.
90   Cass. soc. 29 novembre 1990, *Dr. soc.,* 1991, p.99. Cass. soc. 19 juin 1991, *RJS*, 8-9/1991, n° 959
91   art. L.1234-9 C. trav.
92   art. R.1234-2 C. trav. *Décret* n° 2017-1398 of 25 September 2017 - art.2

in the last 3 months, whichever is the greater.[93] Bonuses and exceptional payments during those times will be included proportionally.

The work contract or collective agreements may set higher compensation. The sum paid will in some circumstances benefit from some exemptions from social contributions, *impôts* and *taxes*.

2) Irregular dismissal (*licenciement irrégulier*) and abusive dismissal (*licenciement abusive*)

An irregular dismissal is one where the employer has failed to respect all or part of the relevant procedure. An abusive dismissal is one where there is no real and serious cause.

a) Sanctions for dismissal with procedural irregularity

Where the error is only one of form or procedure this will not usually itself invalidate the fact that the dismissal is for a real and serious cause. There will usually be no examination of the basis itself for the dismissal, but there will be a claim for damages, with a maximum of 1 month's salary.[94]

b) Sanctions for dismissal without real and serious cause

The judge may order the re-employment of the employee with reinstatement of all accumulated rights and benefits. This is not mandatory; the judge is not obliged to make this order and one or the other party may refuse it.

Where re-employment does not occur, and regardless of any other compensation or indemnities relating to the dismissal, the employer must pay compensation to the employee. The amount of the damages depends upon the length of service. There is a complete scale of amounts in the Code which sets out minimum amounts, and in the case of enterprises usually employing 11 employees or more, there are also maximums. There is a completely separate table of lower minima applicable where the enterprise habitually employs fewer than 11 employees. Generally speaking there is no minimum amount where the employee has been employed for less than 1 year. The minimums start and rise on the scales between:[95]

Fewer than 11 employees:
less than 1 complete year's employment – maximum 1 month's gross salary
1 complete year of employment – half a month's gross salary (maximum 2)
10 years or more of employment – 2 and a half months' gross salary (maximum at that point 10 but rising to 20 after 30 years).

---

93   art. R.1234-4 C. trav. *Décret* n° 2017-1398 of 25 September 2017 - art.3
94   art. L.1235-2 C. trav.
95   art. L.1235-3 C. trav.

11 or more employees:
less than 1 complete year's employment – maximum 1 month's gross salary
1 complete year of employment – 1 month's gross salary (maximum 2)
30 years' employment or more – 3 months' gross salary
   (maximum 20).

Minimum damages will be higher, and usually no less than 6 months' salary, where there was e.g. bullying or harassment involved in the dismissal.

Where the employee has less than 2 years' employment or there are 10 or fewer employees in the enterprise, or where there is no *réelle et sérieuse* cause the compensation is fixed by the judge by virtue of the prejudice caused.[96]

The judge will in addition order the employer to reimburse all or part of any *indemnités de chômage* paid to the employee from the date of the dismissal to the date of the judgment up to a limit of 6 months' of benefits.[97] This will not apply if the employee has less than 2 years of employment or the enterprise has fewer than 11 employees.[98]

c) Damages for dismissal involving harassment, discrimination etc.

Where the dismissal has involved e.g. a breach of a fundamental liberty, bullying, sexual harassment, discrimination or similar, the minimum damages should be 6 months' salary.[99] There is not currently a stated maximum in such cases.

C) Dismissal for economic reasons – *Le licenciement économique*

This is essentially the French law version of redundancy, although there are technical and other differences.

This occurs when an employee is dismissed for reasons not relating to that particular individual, but resulting from a loss or change of the job or a modification refused by the employee of an essential element of the contract resulting mainly from:[100]

1) economic difficulties
Where a significant drop in business, e.g. of orders, is alleged, the periods of time for which such a drop should at least have had an effect for this to count as a justifiable economic reason are broadly:

---

96   art. L.1235-5 C. trav.
97   art. L.1235-4 C. trav.
98   art. L.1235-5 C. trav.
99   art. L.1235-3-1 C. trav.
100 art. L.1233-3 C. trav.

Fewer than 11 employees; a trimester
11 to 49 employees; 2 consecutive trimesters
50 to 299 employees; 3 consecutive trimesters
300 or more employees; 4 consecutive trimesters.

2) technological changes (*mutations technologiques* – technological changes altering the business or how it is done)
3) a re-organisation to protect competitiveness
4) the enterprise ceasing business.

The significance of the loss of change of the job or the modification of the essential element of the contract is assessed at the level of the enterprise.

The significance of the economic difficulties, technological changes or the necessity to safeguard competitiveness of the business are assessed at national level if the enterprise is not part of a group, or otherwise at the level of the common sector of activity of this enterprise and enterprises in the group to which it belongs, established on the national territory.

1) Prevention of dismissals and supporting measures – *Les mésures d'accompagnement*

Dismissal for economic reasons may generally only occur when all efforts at training and adaption have been carried out and *reclassement* of the employee in a job of the same category or equivalent is impossible in the enterprise or in the group of enterprise that it belongs to, situated in the national territory and of which the organisation, the activities or the place of exploitation assure the use of the personnel.[101]

There are various systems and plans that exist to try to avoid employment being lost for these reasons. These include requirements to notify and consult the employees and their representative groups, specific types of plan to try to deal with the situation, and even in some circumstances seeking to find a new owner for the business.

Where the employer is planning to carry out the dismissals for economic reasons, there are additional aids such as the *congé de reclassement*[102] (time off for training, to take steps to seek other work etc.; conditions apply: applicable generally in larger businesses of at least 1,000 employees) and *congé de mobilité*[103] (mobility time off, to help employees return to stable work by seeking assistance, training and work; conditions apply, such as there are minimum employee numbers of 300 set for relevant businesses).

A plan to safeguard the employment – *un plan de sauvegarde de l'emploi* is mandatory in enterprises of 50 employees or more in which the dismissal of

101 art. L.1233-4 C. trav.
102 art. L.1233-71 C. trav.
103 art. L.1237-18 C. trav.

at least 10 employees over 30 days is being looked at. The aim is to avoid the dismissals or to limit the number. It will include a plan to try to place people whose dismissal cannot be avoided in work within the national territory.[104]

Various aspects of the arrangements and the plan may be dealt with by *accord collectif*.[105]

The plan must set out what is intended by way of internal *reclassement* of the employees concerned, creation of new roles within the enterprise, training or *reconversion* (redeployment), as well as any steps including re-organisation of the working time. There are formalities to complete including referral to the *DIRECCTE* (*Direction régionale des entreprises, de la concurrence, de la consommation, du travail et de l'emploi* – Regional authority for businesses, competition, consumption, work and employment).

In enterprises with fewer than 1,000 employees, the employer who is considering dismissal for economic reasons must offer to each of the employees concerned and able to work a *contrat de sécurisation professionnelle* (*CSP*). The employer must inform each employee individually of the existence and contents of the *CSP* during the *entretien préalable* (initial meeting prior to taking steps being considered) or following the last meeting of the representatives of the workers.[106]

The *CSP* effectively terminates the work contract; its aim is the organisation and running of a project for return to work, if applicable by way of redeployment or by a creation or re-taking of an enterprise.[107]

If the employee accepts then they are released from the obligation to work a notice period. They become a trainee and undertake to follow their individual plan organised by *Pôle emploi* (organisation responsible for providing the public service of employment assistance). They will receive an *indemnité de licenciement* and entitlement to certain benefits.

2) Procedures for proposed economic dismissal

Where it is proposed to dismiss fewer than 10 employees in 30 days in an enterprise of at least 11 employees, the employer must initially consult the *CSE*. The *CSE* should provide its opinion in 1 month.[108]

At the meeting, the employer should set out:

1) The economic, financial or technical reasons for the plan
2) The number of dismissals envisaged
3) The professional categories concerned and the proposed criteria for the order of dismissals

---

104 art. L 1233-61 C. trav.
105 art. L.1233 inc. 1233-57-1 C. trav.
106 art. L.1233-66 C. trav.
107 art. L.1233-67 C. trav.
108 art. L.1233-8 and 9 C. trav.

4) The number of employees, permanent or not, employed in the establishment
5) The provisional calendar for the dismissals
6) Economic measures envisaged
7) Where applicable, any consequences that might be expected as a result of the dismissals on health and safety at work.

Where between 1 and fewer than 10 dismissals in 30 days are envisaged, the employer must invite each employee concerned by *LRAR* with no fewer than 5 days' notice to a meeting.[109] At the meeting the employer sets out the reasons and decision envisaged and must listen to the comments of the employee, who is entitled to be assisted at the meeting.

Where the decision is then to dismiss, a set form of *LRAR* should be sent to the employee within (usually) 7 working days of the meeting with reasoned notification of dismissal and an indication of potential priority for re-employment.[110]

The employer must notify the authorities of the dismissal(s) and inform them at various stages of the procedure.

An *accord d'entreprise, de groupe* or *de branche* may set out different arrangements for various procedural aspects of the consultations with the *CSE* or representative bodies but not generally alter the actual rules on consultation.

In enterprises with 50 or more employees the plan and arrangements may be dealt with by an *accord collectif*.[111]

In larger businesses of over 50 employees or where more than 10 dismissals are envisaged over 30 days, the procedure is broadly similar but there will be more meetings.

---

109 art. L.1233-11 C. trav.
110 art. L.1233-15 C. trav.
111 art. L.1233 C. trav.

7. Void/voidable dismissal – *Le licenciement nul*

In certain circumstances (such as when it has been discriminatory) the dismissal may be deemed to be *nul* or void, in which case it will be held to not have occurred, and the contract with all of its terms and effects should be rectified accordingly. The employee must be re-employed in the same or an equivalent job. In certain very limited circumstances the employer may not be obliged to comply with this. The employee may prefer not to do this. If as a result the employee is not taken back on, the judge may order compensation to be paid to them of no less than the salary of the last 6 months.[112]

---

112 art. L.1235-11 C. trav.

8. Fixed term contract – *Contrat de travail à durée déterminée (CDD)*

In principle the treatment of employees on a *CDD* should be equal to that of employees on a *CDI* although the rules relating to termination of the contract will be different.[113] Generally the rules applicable will be the same unless specified to the contrary.

Fixed term contracts are subject to more formalities. Such a contract must be in writing, failing which the contract will be deemed to be a *CDI*.[114]

The contract must also contain the necessary information. There are also circumstances where a *CDD* may not be allowed or there may be maximum durations allowed, etc.

Where the contract is re-classified as a *CDI* (*requalification-sanction*) the employer must also pay a penalty to the employee of not less than 1 month's salary.

A) Clauses

Certain specific clauses must be in the contract, including:[115]

- the fact that it is a *CDD à objet défini*

- name and reference of any *accord/convention collectif* responsible for the contract

- exact definition of its purpose

- its intended length

- details of the tasks which the contract is for

- details of the name and qualification of the person who is being replaced where applicable

---

113 art. L.1242-14 C. trav.
114 art. L.1242-12 C. trav.
115 art. L.1242-12, al. 1er C. trav.

- designation of the post and, where applicable, if it is on the list of work presenting particular risks to health or safety provided in art. L.4154-2 of the *Code du travail*, designation of the work, or where the contract is to assure an addition to the work training of the employee in compliance with art. L.1242-3 of the *Code du travail*, designation of the nature of the activities

- the event or result which concludes the contract

- length of any *périod d'essai* if applicable

- amount of remuneration and its different compositions, including where applicable any bonuses or benefits

- conditions of notice period and of potential renewal if applicable

- a clause setting out the possibility of termination on the anniversary date of the conclusion of the contract, by either party, for a real and serious reason. The right of the employee, when this termination is by the employer, to an indemnity equal to 10% of the gross total remuneration of the employee (N.B. this indemnity provision does not apply to all types of employment and may also be reduced by *accord collectif* or denied if for example the employee unreasonably refuses an offer to transform the *CDD* into a *CDI*)

- the name and address of the *caisse de retraite complèmentaire* as well as, where relevant, those of the *organisme de prévoyance*.

B) Trial period – *Période d'essai*

Where a probationary period is included, it must be proportionate to the length of the contract. Unless either custom or *conventions* sets out lower durations, the period should not exceed 1 day per week of the contract up to limits of:[116]

Contract not greater than 6 months – 2 weeks
Contract exceeds 6 months – 1 month.

Where the contract does not contain a precise term, the duration of the *période d'éssai* will be calculated using the minimum possible length of the contract.

---

116 art. L.1242-10 C. trav.

Where the *période d'éssai* is at least 1 week, termination of the contract must be preceded by a *délai de prévenance*, which will again depend upon the length of attendance of the employee.[117]

C) Circumstances for which a *CDD* may not be used

- to replace an employee who is not working because of a *conflit collectif* (generally speaking, on strike)[118]

- to carry out particularly dangerous works that are set out in a list[119]

- to fulfil a temporary growth need resulting from the enterprise having dismissed employees for economic reasons in the preceding 6 months[120] (this may however be allowed if the *CDD* is for less than 3 months and is not renewable, or is related to certain exceptional exportation works and in that case also subject to complying with formalities related to consultation with the *CSE* (if it exists)

- Generally, once any potential renewals have reached their end, successive *CDDs* may only be allowed after the expiration of a delay period between the contracts. For contracts agreed after the publication of the *ordonnance n° 2017-1387 du 22 septembre 2017*, the delay periods may be set by a *convention* or *un accord de branche étendu* but if not are set out in the Code and depend upon the length of the *CDD* that has expired.[121]

For contracts agreed after the publication of the *ordonnance n° 2017-1387 du 22 septembre 2017*, a *convention* or *un accord de branche étendu* may set out where a delay period is not required.[122] Where that has not been done, there are set circumstances where the intervening delay is not required, e.g. where the contract has been to replace a temporarily absent employee who then has a new absence; or where the new contract is required for carrying out urgent security measures; or certain seasonal works or work where the *CDD* has become the usual form of contract due to the temporary nature of the work.[123]

---

117 art. L.1221-25 C. trav.
118 art. L.1242-6, 1° C. trav.
119 art. L.1242-6, 2° C. trav.
120 art. L.1242-5 C. trav.
121 art. L.1244-3 C. trav.
122 art. L.1244-4 C. trav.
123 art. L.1244-4 C. trav.

D) Circumstances where a *CDD* may be used

A *CDD* may only be used where there is a specific temporary task and in situations authorised by law, e.g.:

- the replacement of another employee who is temporarily absent[124]

- for the replacement of an employee as a temporary measure for a change to part-time work, by an addition to the usual contract of an employee
- for the replacement of an employee who has been suspended

- for the intervening period (and subject to any relevant consultations) after an employee has left permanently but prior to the intended removal of the post

- to fill in an absence prior to the start of the employment of a person who has been recruited on a *CDI*

- temporary growth in the activity of the business[125]

- necessity to carry out urgent safety works

- work that is temporary by nature (e.g. seasonal work, and/or fruit-picking) or work where the *CDD* has become the usual form of contract due to the temporary nature of the work [126]

- certain other roles such as the head of certain types of business or a person who is for example in a *profession libérale*, family assistants, certain agricultural workers etc., as set out in the provisions of art. L.1242-2 4° and 5° of the *Code du travail*

- for the recruitment of certain classes of employee for work usually used for a particular project[127] e.g. for engineers and *cadres*, for which the use has recently been extended by changes to the law. There must be provision for such a contract in an *accord de branche étendu* or if not by an *accord d'entreprise*. These contracts are subject to various other strict regulations. This might for example be used to arrange an additional period of work for a person at the end of their career to enable them to reach the required length of employment to entitle them to full retirement benefits. (N.B. A certain

---

124 art. L.1242-2, 1° C. trav.
125 art. L.1242-2, 2° C. trav.
126 art. L.1242-2, 3° C. trav.
127 art. L.1242-2, 6° C. trav.

type of contract is coming into existence known as a *contrat de projet*. This may technically be a *CDI* and is likely to be an extension of the *CDI de chantier*, which is a type of contract used for the purposes of a fixed piece of work but for which the time necessary is not certain. This type of contract will not usually lead to an entitlement to the *prime de précarité* at its end, being used specifically to enable employers to make contracts that have an ending at the conclusion of the particular project.)

There are certain other limited exceptional uses, for example to assist where there is a legal obligation to improve the employment opportunities for certain categories of people or to complete legal requirements to ensure a certain amount of professional development training to an employee[128] or at the end of apprenticeship contracts in certain limited specified circumstances only.[129]

E) Determining the duration, number of renewals and delay between contracts

Recent reforms allow for these to be set by *convention* or *accord de branche* for contracts agreed after the publication of *ordonnance n° 2017-1387 du 22 septembre 2017*.[130] Where neither exists, the provisions set out in the Code will apply. This also applies to *contrats à l'intérim*.

F) Duration of a *CDD*

A *CDD* may be either for a set term (*un terme précis*) or not (*sans terme précis*). In the first case, the duration and start and end dates must be set out in the contract. In the second case, the event causing the ending of the contract must be set out in the contract.

Where there is no *convention* or *accord de branche*, *CDD à terme précis* should generally not exceed:[131]

18 months (including any renewals). This is reduced to 9 months where a person is recruited pending the appointment of a person on a *CDI*, or for urgent safety works.

---

128 art. L.1242-3 C. trav.
129 art. L.1242-4 C. trav.
130 E.g. art. L.1242-8 C. trav.
131 art. L.1242-8-1 C. trav.

24 months if the employment is to be carried out abroad, or where an employee is leaving prior to their post being totally terminated, or in the event of an exceptional export order. In the latter case a usual initial minimum term of 6 months will apply and prior to any such recruitments the employer must consult with the *CSE* if it exists. N.B. this provision is slightly different to that which applies to contracts agreed prior to the publication of *ordonnance n° 2017-1387 du 22 septembre 2017*.

No less than 18 months and no more than 36 months for the specific type of contract used by e.g. engineers or *cadres* for work on a particular project (as set out above[132]). In this case it may not be renewed.

When a *CDD sans terme précis* is used there should at least be a minimum term. In default, the contract will be reclassified as a *CDI*.[133] The *CDD* ends when the determining event occurs (e.g. the return to work of the employee who has been temporarily absent).[134]

G) Successive *CDD*s

The number of renewals for contracts agreed after publication of *ordonnance n° 2017-1387 du 22 septembre 2017* may be set by *convention* or *accord de branche*. In the absence of this, then generally *CDD* may be renewed twice,[135] subject always to article L.1242-8 of the *Code du travail*. This possibility does not apply to *CDD*s that are for the purpose of aiding certain categories of people seeking employment or to help employees complete a level of professional qualification.[136]

Renewals of the *CDD* are not the same as having successive ones. Normally speaking, if the work continues after the *CDD* ends, the contract becomes a *CDI*.[137]

Certain categories of contract such as those to replace an absent employee whose absence is extended, or on suspension, or seasonal work etc. may however be renewed.[138]

Apart from these exceptions to the usual rule on continuation of the contract, there must usually be a break between renewals or before re-employment on any other type of temporary work contract. This is a *délai de carence*.

---

132 art. L.1242-8-2 C. trav.
133 art. L.1242-8 6° C. trav.
134 art. L.1242-7 C. trav.
135 art. L.1243-13 C. trav.
136 art. L.1243-13 C. trav.
137 art. L.1243-11 C. trav.
138 arts. L.1244-1 and L.1244-2 C. trav.

The duration of the *délai de carence* is calculated by reference to the length of the *CDD* (including any renewals). Where the contract was agreed after the publication of *ordonnance n° 2017-1387 du 22 septembre 2017* the delays and the circumstances in which they may/may not be used may be set by *convention* or *accord de branche*. In the absence of such agreements the following rules will usually apply:[139]

- *CDD* less than 14 days – *délai* half of the length of the *CDD* including any renewal

- *CDD* equal to or greater than 14 days – *délai* one-third of the length of the *CDD* including any renewal.

Only days on which the business is open are included in the calculation, i.e. not calendar days.

If the *délai* is not respected, the contract will be re-qualified as a *CDI*.

There are certain circumstances where (in the absence of the agreements referred to above) no *délai* is required, e.g.:[140]

- the employee who is being replaced is absent again

- urgent safety works are required

- seasonal work or *CDD d'usage*

- certain heads of businesses or those in a *profession libérale*

- *CDDs* which are used for the purpose of aiding certain categories of people seeking employment or to help employees complete a level of professional qualification

- where the employee has terminated the contract early (*rupture anticipée*)

- when the employee has refused the renewal of the contract, for the period of the contract that has not been renewed.

---

139 art. L.1244-3 to L.1244-4 C. trav.
140 art. L.1244-4 C. trav.

H) Termination (*rupture*) at the end of a *CDD*

No further formality is required once a *CDD* reaches the end of its term or defining event; it simply ceases. The employee may have a right to pay for leave untaken.

If the contract is not renewed or replaced by another by that employer, the employee will be entitled to a payment from the employer known as *une indemnité de fin de contrat/indemnité de précarité*,[141] which is intended to compensate them for the insecurity of the arrangement. The payment is 10% of the gross sum received by the employee during their contract. This may be limited by *accord de branche étendu* (agreement between all the employers and representatives of the employees in a given sector of work) or *accord d'entreprise* (agreement between the employer and the representatives of the employees/union there) down to 6% if professional training is offered to the employee in place of the balance of the payment.[142]

The *indemnité de fin de contrat* is not payable in certain circumstances including:

- seasonal work or other work sectors where it is the custom to have a *CDD*

- *CDD*s which are used for the purpose of aiding certain categories of people seeking employment or to help employees complete a level of professional qualification

- where the employee is a young person working during their school or university holidays

- the employee has refused a *CDI* offered by the employer for a similar job

- where the *CDD* is broken by the employee, or by the employer for *faute* or in case of *force majeure*.

I) Termination of the contract before the point of its end date

It is generally not possible to end a *CDD* prior to its conclusion except in certain circumstances set out in article L.1343-1 of the *Code du travail*:

- agreement of the parties

---

141 art. L.1243-8 C. trav.
142 art. L.1243-9 C. trav.

- *faute grave*

- *force majeure*

- the employee is declared unfit for the work by a work doctor.

The employee may end the *CDD* before its term subject to giving applicable notice to enable them to enter into a *CDI*.[143]

Where the *CDD* is ended early without one of the above situations by the employee, then the employer is entitled to claim damages and interest for any loss occasioned.[144]

Where it is ended early by the employer outside the above situations, the employee is entitled to claim damages and interest for at least the total remuneration they would have received had the contract been completed to its conclusion, without prejudice to the *indemnité de précarité*. They will not have this entitlement if the termination by the employer is for *faute grave* by the employee, *force majeure* or medical unfitness confirmed by the work's doctor. If the cause of the termination is *force majeure,* the employee is entitled to a payment equal to the amount of the remunerations that they would have received until the end of the contract.[145]

If the unfitness results from a cause that is not work-related then the employee will be entitled to a payment for termination of the *CDD* of an amount equal to at least the legal entitlement on dismissal.[146]

If the unfitness results from a work-related cause then the employee is entitled to payment equal to at least double the legal entitlement on dismissal.[147]

In either case, the termination of the *CDD* may only take place following an attempt to find the employee alternative employment.

In some circumstances a judge may order that the contract should be completed by the parties including the employee carrying out the work.[148]

Early termination of a *CDD* can also give rise to criminal penalties.

J) Indemnity for employment insecurity – *Indemnité de précarité*

The employee is usually, but not always entitled to this payment at the end of the contract, however it will not usually be required if the contract

---

143 art. L.1243-2 C. trav.
144 art. L.1243-3 C. trav.
145 art. L.1243-4 C. trav.
146 art. L.1226-4-3 C. trav.
147 art. L.1226-20 C. trav.
148 Soc. 6 févr. 2013 *Dalloz actualité, 27 févr. 2013, obs. Ines; Dr. Soc. 2013. 415, note Mouly*

ends during a trial period. It will also not be required for e.g. some seasonal contracts, or if for example the employee refuses an offer to continue the *CDD* after its term on a *CDI*.

9. Some particular types of contract

A) Apprenticeship – *Contrat d'apprentissage*

With an apprenticeship contract, the employer undertakes to pay a salary to a worker, previously usually aged 16 and 25 years old, and to provide them with a training given by the enterprise and by an apprentice training centre (*centre de formation des apprentis/CFA*).

There are rules allowing adjustment of the age limits in certain cases, for example:

- people aged 15 years old may also enter into such a contract provided they have completed the third year of secondary school (*troisième*)[149]

- the age limit has been increased to up to 30 in certain cases (where the apprentice has signed a new contract leading to a qualification superior to the present one, and where the previous contract has been interrupted but not by the choice of the apprentice) and as a temporary experimental measure separately in certain geographical areas[150] (Bretagne; Bourgogne-Franche-Comté; Centre-Val de Loire; Grand Est ; Hauts-de-France; Ile de France; Occitanie; Nouvelle-Aquitaine; Pays de la Loire) by recent reforms, to allow for greater use of this type of contract.

The worker undertakes to work for the enterprise and to complete the training.

There are particular rules and procedures that must be respected for this type of contract that are quite detailed.

1) Formalities
This type of contract must for example be in writing and signed by the parties[151] and there are various elements that must be set out, including the

---

149 art. R.6221-1 C. trav.
150 Décret n° 2016-1998 du 30 décembre 2016 fixant la liste des collectivités territoriales autorisées à participer aux expérimentations prévues aux articles 76 et 77 de la loi n° 2016-1088 du 8 août 2016 relative au travail, à la modernisation du dialogue social et à la sécurisation des parcours professionnels
151 art. L.6222-4 C. trav.

title of the qualification, the name of the *CFA* where the employee is registered and the name of the person or people to whom they will be apprenticed (*maîtres d'apprentissage*). It may be necessary to obtain prior consent of relevant authorities before entering into the contract.

2) Length of the contract
The contract may be a *CDD* or a *CDI*. If for a fixed term, it will usually be between 1 and 3 years.[152]

3) Termination of the *Contrat d'apprentissage*[153]
The contract may be terminated without notice or penalty by either party during the first 45 days.

After the first 45 days the contract may usually only be terminated by express written mutual consent of the parties, or in certain cases by an order (*résiliation judiciaire*) obtained from the *conseil de prud'hommes*. In either case, the termination must be notified to the director of the relevant *CFA*.

B) Work experience placement – *Stage*

There is provision under the *Code de l'éducation*[154] for schools and universities to include work experience placements as part of their courses. These placements are not usually classified as employment in the same way as apprenticeships and other professional training schemes as set out in art. L.4153-1 of the *Code du travail*; they are viewed more as part of educational experience. However, they do benefit from various protections in the *Code du travail*.

These placements are strictly regulated. The contract itself should be created using a particular form and should not usually exceed 6 months per academic year. The contract can be a *CDD* or a *CDI*.

Where the period exceeds 2 months consecutively or 2 months non-consecutively but within the same academic year, the employee is entitled to a payment referred to as a *gratification* (which is not treated the same way as a salary) which is fixed according to *convention de branche* or *accord professionnel étendu* or if not, set scales.

---

152 art. L.6222-7-1 C. trav.
153 art. L.6222-18 C. trav.
154 art. L.124 C. l'éd.

C) Contract for professional qualification – *Contrat de professionalisation*[155]

There are rules setting out the use of contracts for particular work/professional qualifications that involve both studies and periods of work experience of the relevant job in order to learn how to do it and providing protections. There are age and situational criteria that will usually apply because the contract is particularly aimed at assisting people who are not yet/currently in employment obtain work experience leading to qualifications.

The contract itself should be created using a particular form. It can be a *CDD* or a *CDI*.

The contract will usually be for 6 to 12 months but there are circumstances in which they can be for as long as 24 months.

Employees under these contracts are entitled to be paid at least set minimum amounts (usually taken from the *SMIC – Salaire minimum interprofessionnel de croissance* – which is a scale of minimum wages) which are generally related to the age of the employee and their level of qualification.

D) Contract for people aged over 57 – *CDD senior*[156]

This is a type of contract intended to aid the return to work of a person aged over 57 years and to allow them to accumulate additional rights relating to their retirement. It may be part time or full time.

1) Conditions for use

This is not available in agricultural industries. The contract may be for any person over 57 years old registered as seeking work for more than 3 months or subject to a *convention de reclassement personnalisé* (a type of procedure that has been offered by the employer to an employee facing dismissal by the employer on economic grounds, intended to assist them in re-qualifying for or finding other work or to complete work necessary to acquire full pension rights).

2) Length

This type of contract must be a *CDD à terme précis* of no more than 18 months, although it may be renewed once for a maximum further 18 months.[157] No period of break is required between succeeding contracts.

---

155 arts. L.6325 and D.6325 C. trav.
156 art. D.1242-2 C. trav.
157 art. D.1242-7 C. trav.

E) Other types of *CDD*

There are various other types of *CDD* that are intended to assist people in various different ways in returning to the workforce. These are known as *contrats d'insertion* or *contrats aides*. Examples might be:

- *Contrat unique d'insertion (CUI)*[158]

- *Emploi d'avenir*[159]

- *Emploi d'avenir professeur*[160]

- *Contrat adultes-relais*[161]

- *Garantie jeunes.*[162]

Each of these types of contract is regulated and should comply with the relevant rules and formalities.

---

158 art. L.5134-19 C. trav.
159 art. L.5134-100-112 C. trav.
160 art. L.5134-120-129 C.trav.
161 art. L.5134-100-109 C. trav.
162 art. L.5131-6 C. trav.

10. Temporary work contracts – *Contrat de travail temporaire (intérimaire) – CTT*

The *CTT* is used where an employee is provided on a temporary basis by a temporary work agency to a client for the execution of a mission.[163]

This involves the conclusion of 2 separate contracts:

1. a commercial contract, the contract between the temporary work enterprise (*entreprise de travail temporaire – ETT*) and between the client enterprise (*le contrat de mise à disposition*)

2. the work contract between the temporary work agency and the employee, the worker (*le contrat de mission*).

There are certain circumstances in which this type of contract may be used (to which as usual there are some exceptions) and these are set out in the Code and include:[164]

- the replacement of another employee who is temporarily absent

- for the replacement of an employee as a temporary measure for a change to part-time work, by an addition to the usual contract of an employee

- for the replacement of an employee who has been suspended

- for the intervening period (and subject to consultation with the *CSE* if it exists) after an employee has left permanently but prior to the intended removal of the post

- to fill in an absence prior to the start of the employment of a person who has been recruited on a *CDI*

---

163 art. L.1251-1 C. trav.
164 art. L.1251-6 C. trav.

- temporary growth in the activity of the business

- work that is temporary by nature (e.g. seasonal work, fruit-picking) or work where the *CDD* has become the usual form of contract due to the temporary nature of the work

- certain other roles such as the head of certain types of business or a person who is for example in a *profession libérale,* family assistants, certain agricultural workers etc.

- there are certain other limited exceptional uses, for example to assist where there is a legal obligation to improve the employment opportunities for certain categories of people or to complete legal requirements to ensure a certain amount of professional development training to an employee or at the end of apprenticeship contracts in certain limited specified circumstances only.

This type of employment should not be used to replace a worker whose contract is suspended following a *conflit collectif* or for certain specified dangerous works or to replace a work's doctor.[165]

There are also restrictions on the use of temporary employees in the 6 months following any dismissals for *motif économique* although in some limited circumstances it may be allowed.[166]

The employment contract should be in writing and mandatory clauses should be included such as the following:[167]

- the contents of the *mise à disposition*

- the "professional qualification" of the employee; this refers to a system used in France to organise a sort of hierarchy of work which will be used for assessing e.g. the levels of salaries and other rights

- the details of the remuneration and method of remuneration of the employee, including the *indemnité à fin de mission*
  length of any trial period

- if the contract is to be performed in another country, a clause that the employee will be repatriated at the expense of the employer. This clause will not apply if the employee terminates the contract early

---

165 art. L.1251-10 C. trav.
166 art. L.1251-9 C. trav.
167 art. L.1251-16 C. trav.

- name and address of the relevant *caisse de retraite complémentaire* and the *organisme prévoyance*

- clause that the employment of the employee by the user

- business at the end of the mission is not forbidden.

Any clause seeking to forbid the client company from recruiting the employee is null.

Duration and probationary periods

Recent reforms allow for the length of these contracts where agreed after the publication of *ordonnance n° 2017-1387 du 22 septembre 2017*, the number of renewals, and any delay between successive contracts, to be set by *accord de branche* or *convention*.[168] Where neither exists, the usual laws will apply as follows:

The total duration including any renewals of a *contrat de mission*[169] should not usually exceed 18 months.

It shall be:

9 months where it is in anticipation of the arrival of an employee on a *CDI* or where urgent security measures are needed.

24 months where the work is abroad, or where it is to replace an employee who has left and whose post is to be removed, where there is an exceptional export order (in which case the minimum period is 6 months).

36 months in certain particular circumstances relating to the period of certain apprenticeships.

Usually a probationary period[170] should be included only where the length has been set by a *convention de branche étendu* or *accord d'entreprise ou d'établissement*.

In default of an applicable agreement setting duration, the duration of any probationary period is set out in the Code and will depend upon the duration of the task, and vary between 2 and 5 days. It is calculated in calendar days, but not including bank holidays and other set/obligatory rest days.

Where the job to be carried out is equal to or less than 1 month, the maximum duration for a probationary period is 2 days.

Where the job is more than 1 month and equal to or less than 2 months, the maximum duration is 3 days.

Where the job is for longer than 2 months, the maximum is 5 days.

168 art. L.1251-12 C. trav.
169 art. L.1251-12-1 C. trav.
170 art. L.1251-14 C. trav.

Authorised use and penalties for misuse

Circumstances where the use of such contracts is allowed, or forbidden, governing successive contracts for the same job and penalties for misuse are generally the same as for a *CDD*.

Rights of temporary workers

The conditions of work of the temporary worker are the responsibility of the business within which the employee is based. Broadly speaking, the employee is entitled to the same rights and remuneration as an employee in the same position would have in the business.

This will include with regard to:[171]

- the length of the work

- night work

- weekly time off and bank holidays

- health and safety

- rights relating to women, children and *jeunes travailleurs*

The temporary agency (and not the client company) will retain responsibility for disciplinary action and the requirement to provide the services of a work doctor.[172]

Any rights from collective agreements arise from those relating to the *ETT* only.

Termination of the contract

At the end of the contract, the *ETT* must pay a sum to the employee known as *une indemnité de fin de mission* which must equal at least 10% of the gross remuneration paid to the employee for that task. This sum will not be due if the employee is then recruited by the client enterprise, or if the temporary work contract is terminated for *faute grave* or by the employee.

If the employee terminates the contract early the *ETT* would be entitled to damages and interest for loss/damage caused, unless the employee has done this because they have obtained a *CDI*. The employee should give notice, which is broadly speaking usually of 1 day per week of the contract/period worked if a *CDI*, subject to an overall minimum of 1 day and maximum of 2 weeks.[173]

---

171 art. L.1251-21 C. trav.
172 art. L.1251-22 C. trav.
173 art. L.1251-28 C. trav.

If the contract is terminated by the *ETT* and there has been no *faute grave* or *force majeure*, the *ETT* must within 3 working days from the termination offer the employee a new contract for an equivalent task. Up to 3 supplementary contracts may be used to do this. If no new contract is offered in the set time or if the new contract(s) is(/are) for less than the remaining term of the original contract, the *ETT* would be obliged to pay the employee a sum equivalent to the sum the employee would have received if the contract had been continued for its full term including any *indemnités* due at the end.[174]

---

174 art. L.1251-26 C. trav.

11. Remuneration – *Rémuneration*

A) Constituents

This may include the basic salary (whatever basis it is calculated on, e.g. time, per task etc.) and all other benefits, e.g. bonuses, allowances etc. (*primes*), benefits in kind etc.

The value of all of these is added together for the calculation of social contributions. Benefits in kind will have values allocated by *conventions collectives*, by custom (*usage*) or by the work contract.

B) Setting the level of salary (*salaire*)

The amount of the salary may be chosen freely by the parties but must respect any relevant laws or *conventions*, the contract itself and relevant customs/practices.

C) Non-discrimination

In principle, all workers in the same situation who have the same skills and qualifications should be paid equally by their employer: "*à travail égal, salaire égal*" – equal work, equal salary.

A particular example of this codified expressly is that men and women must be paid equally for all work of equal value.[175]

The burden of proof of inequality lies with the employee alleging it.

D) Minimum wage – *Salaire minimum interprofessionnel de croissance (SMIC)*

An hourly minimum wage is set annually on 1 January which will generally be applicable to all employees, whether full time or part time, on a *CDI* or a *CDD*.

There are certain exceptions; *assistants maternelles*, *jeunes* aged under 18,

---

175 arts. L.3221.1 et 2 C. trav.

apprentissages and *contrats de professionalisation*, *stagiaires*, those on certain types of *contrats aidés* and non-exclusive *VRP* (*Voyageur, représentant, et placier* – a French term for a class of salaried sales representatives).

When calculating the salary received for this purpose, all remuneration, bonuses etc. directly related to the work carried out are included in the total. Supplementary sums paid that are not directly related to the work carried out are not included (e.g. additional payments for night shift work, because of long service).

E) Any minimum set by *convention collective*

The employer may not pay less than the amount due to the employee according to their position in the scale of remuneration set by the *convention*, even if the employee agrees. The amount paid may be higher.

The *convention* may set out what should be included in the calculation of the salary, but in default then the calculation would be as for the *SMIC*.

F) Payment of the salary

Payment will usually be made monthly[176] although certain categories of employment do not always follow this, e.g. employees working at home, seasonal workers, various temporary workers. For such workers, they should be paid at least twice a month, at no more than 16-day intervals.[177]

A wage slip (*bulletin de salaire*) must be provided when each payment is made.[178] Copies should be kept by the parties for at least 3 years, the limitation for claims for many of the sums due from the employer being generally 3 years. This time limit runs either from the end of the contract if it has been ended, or if not from the date on which the claimant knew or ought to have known of the facts leading to the claim.[179]

G) Union negotiation timings

Where an enterprise has at least 1 relevant union and/or at least 1 *délégué syndical* (generally speaking, those with at least 50 employees) there must be pay negotiations at least once every 4 years.

---

176 art. L.3242-1 C. trav.
177 art. L.3242-3 C. trav.
178 art. L.3243-2 C. trav.
179 art. L.3245-1 C. trav.

The negotiations must cover 2 broad themes:

- the remuneration, working time and the allocation of "value added" (this refers to the value added by the business as a result of its work. The allocation of the value added in this case refers to how this value added is apportioned between the various participants/means of participating in the business, e.g. salaries and dividends)

- equality between men and women and the quality of life at work.

H) Contractual clauses for changes to remuneration

Such clauses are permissible but must be based upon objective elements independent of the wishes of the employer; the clause must not place the risk of the business on the employee, and they must not have the effect of reducing the remuneration below the *SMIC* or the minimum set by *convention*.[180] Furthermore, the agreement of the employee to a change to remuneration is required even where the change is advantageous.[181]

I) Financial participation of employees – *Participation financière des salariés*

1) *L'intéressement*

This is a non-mandatory form of participation scheme. It provides tax advantages to the paying employer and to the receiving employee provided that it and its use comply with certain requirements.[182]

It is calculated by reference to the performance of the enterprise[183] and therefore will tend to be variable. Where the scheme is set up it must operate in a non-discriminatory way.

Setting up and calculation of the *intéressement*
The agreement is made for 3 years by:[184]

1) a *convention* or *accord collectif de travail*
2) agreement between the employer and the representatives of the unions in that enterprise
3) agreement with the *CSE*

---

180 Cass. soc. 2 juillet 2002, *Dr. soc.*, 2002, p. 998
181 Cass. Soc. 8 juin 2016, n° 15-10.116
182 art. L.3312 C. trav.
183 art. L.3312-1 C. trav.
184 art. L.3312-5 C. trav.

4) ratification by a majority of two-thirds of the personnel of a draft agreement put forward by the employer. If there is 1 or more union representatives or a *CSE* then the ratification must be asked for by the employer and 1 or more of the unions or the *CSE*.

Formalities apply to these agreements.[185] The agreement must contain particular clauses including amongst others:

- the time for which the *intéressement* is agreed and the date of its taking effect

- the establishment(s) concerned

- procedures to be used

- calculation methods and the criteria for distribution of the *intéressement*

- dates for payments

- conditions under which the *CSE* or a commission specially created by it obtains necessary information about the conditions for the application of the contractual clauses

- procedures for dealing with any disputes that might arise in the application of or amendment of the agreement.

The *intéressement* must result from a formula taking into account the results of the business or performance criteria.[186] It may not be used to replace any part of the obligatory remuneration.

The total of the benefits that may be paid[187] is limited annually to 20% of the gross salaries and where applicable of the annual remuneration or professional income that was subject to income tax of the beneficiaries referred to in art. L.3312-3 (e.g. heads of businesses or presidents etc.) for the previous year paid to the people concerned.

The amount paid to each employee may not exceed half of the annual limit of the sum withheld for the calculation of social security payments.

If the sums are placed by the employee into such a regulated *plan d'épargne entreprise* then if they take sums from it within time limits set by regulations, the sums will benefit from exemptions from income tax up to half the average limit of the deductions for social security.[188]

---

185 art. L.3313-1 C. trav., art. L.3313-2 C. trav.
186 art. L.3314-2 C. trav.
187 art. L.3314-8 C. trav.
188 art. L.3315-2 C. trav.

12. Profit sharing – *Participation aux résultats*

This is a type of investment scheme. The intention is to involve the employees in the growth of the enterprise.[189] Specific relevant sums that are payable to the employee are instead locked in for 5 years (the employee has a short opportunity to claim immediate payment of the sums but this does not benefit from the same tax advantage). They are calculated by reference to various factors including the results of the enterprise, the amount of its capital, and value added. The sums that are paid into the scheme will at the time of payment to the employee after the locked-in period be exempt from income tax and – from the perspective of the business – are deductible from its taxable sums. They are also not taken into account for social security calculations.[190]

The scheme does not apply to all types of business (depending for example on the degree of State ownership). However, for most companies, where there have been normally at least 50 employees for at least 12 months (consecutive or not) in the last 3 years, participation becomes mandatory.[191] For most businesses that are not covered by the mandatory rules, including for example employers with fewer than 50 employees over the relevant period, the scheme may be set up by agreement.[192]

All employees are included, however a degree of continuous employment may be required (not to exceed 3 months).[193]

A) Setting up the scheme

The preliminary step is an *accord de participation* that will usually last 3 years. It may include joining a *plan salarial d'épargne interentreprises*. It may be a result of either a *convention* or an *accord collectif du travail*, an *accord d'entreprise* between the employer and the union representatives in the enterprise, an *accord* made by

---

189 art. L.3322-1 C. trav.
190 art. L.3325 C. trav.
191 art. L.3322-2 C. trav.
192 art. L 3312-2 C. trav.
193 art. L.3342-1 C. trav.

the *CSE* or by ratification by a two-thirds majority of an agreement proposed by the employer. If there is 1 or more union representatives or a *CSE* then the ratification must be asked for by the employer and 1 or more of the unions or the *CSE*.[194]

It must contain certain mandatory clauses including:[195]

- start and end date

- the establishment(s) that it applies to

- procedures to be used

- the methods to be used for calculating the sums involved and criteria for its distribution

- the payment dates

- conditions under which the *CSE* or a commission specially created by it obtains the necessary information about the conditions for the application of the contractual clauses

- how disputes regarding the scheme or any amendment will be dealt with.

The agreement must be lodged with the relevant administrative authority within a set period.

B) Calculation and sharing of the *réserve spéciale de participation*

1) Basic formula

A basic formula is set out in the *Code du travail*.[196] Agreements may use different calculations but the benefit to the employee should be at least equal to that.[197]

---

194 art. L.3312-5 C. trav.
195 art. L.3313-2 C. trav.
196 art. L.3324 C. trav.
197 art. L.3324-2 C. trav.

2) Restriction of rights/access to funds over a certain time period

Each year the employee has a choice to:

- block the funds for 5 years
- ask for the immediate payment of all or part of the share; this would however disentitle the employee to the tax exemption that would apply to the benefit.

Employees' funds may be released early in certain circumstances, including for example:[198]

- invalidity
- retirement
- death.

It is also possible to allow participation by the granting of shares, or by the granting of the right to obtain shares or *certificats d'investissement* (a type of share) at a set price.

There are various other types of saving schemes (*épargnes salariales*) for employees to use within a business which may also involve the locking-in of sums for a period, but will generally have more limited financial benefits. These may come in various forms, such as the *épargne salariale d'entreprise* (*PEE*) or the *plan d'épargne pour la retraite collectif* (*Perco*).

---

198 art. R.3332-29 C. trav.

13. Work time – *Durée de travail*

The effective working time (*temps de travail effectif – durée effectif*) is defined as being the time during which the employee is at the disposition of the employer and must comply with the employer's orders without having the power to freely set about their private occupations.[199] There is a presumption that time spent inside the enterprise is working time.

There are numerous examples of what may or may not count as work time; for example, the following will usually be included as working time:

- travel time between different work sites

- additional work travel that is not carried out in usual working hours

- time spent actually working by employee who is on call – i.e. not the whole of the time on call (time spent on call is known as *le temps d'astreinte* and an employee on call is *sous astreinte*).[200]

Time spent eating and drinking and rest times may nevertheless count as work time if in the circumstances the time fulfils the definition of *temps de travail effectif*.

Remuneration for time spent on food/drinks, and rest pauses that count as work time may be agreed by *convention*, by *accord d'entreprise* or *d'établissement* or an *accord de branch* even in circumstances where they would not usually count as work time.[201] The *accord* would set out the methods of organisation of the financial compensation or time off in lieu.

Time changing into and from work outfits that are required by the employment will usually be the subject of recompense either by money or by rest period.[202] A *convention*, *accord d'entreprise* or *d'établissement* or an *accord de branch* may be used either to set the recompense or to the time as part of the *temps de travail effectif*, and also to set the recompense for time spent travelling to and from work where the time involved exceeds the normal.[203] In the case

---

199 art. L.3121-1 C. trav.
200 art. L.3121-9 C. trav.
201 art. L.3121-6 C. trav.
202 art. L.3121-3 C. trav.
203 art. L.3121-7 C. trav.

of the travelling time, the employer arranges the conditions after information and consultation with the *CSE*.[204]

If there is no *accord* as set out above, the contract may set out remuneration for food and drink breaks and rest. The contract may also set out recompense for time changing to and from work outfits, or the contract may define that time as part of work time.[205]

Time spent *sous astreinte* may be compensated by either payment or by rest time. Reasonable notice must be given to employees of any times for being on call.[206]

The phrase *amplitude journalière* includes effective working time as defined, plus breaks, meal times and interruptions.

Most employees are deemed to have a usual hourly working time per period, known as the *durée légale*, beyond which for a full-time employee any additional hours worked are known as *heures supplémentaires*, which are subject to particular rules (see separate section below) or for a part-time employee are known as *heures complémentaire*, which are subject to separate rules (see separate section below). Where additional hours are worked, they give rise to rights to additional remuneration, or sometimes additional rest time.

Recent legal changes have made it simpler for businesses to organise Sunday work, and to allow slightly more flexibility to be brought in by employers over the start and end of night hours.

A) Maximum working period – *Durée maximale du travail*

Minimum rest times – *Durée minimale de repos*

Once daily work time reaches 6 hours, employees are generally entitled to a rest period of at least 20 consecutive minutes.[207] For *jeunes travailleurs* the work period should not exceed 4 and a half hours, following which a break of 30 consecutive minutes should be given.[208]

All employees must have at least 11 consecutive hours of rest per day. Otherwise phrased, the *amplitude journalière maximale* (maximum working day length) may not normally exceed 13 hours. This may be altered in urgent situations or where decrees allow. It may also be reduced by *une convention* or *accord d'entreprise* or *d'établissement* or if none, by *convention* or *accord de branche* is allowed by decree in certain circumstances, for example to allow continuity of service, and in certain circumstances of a sudden increase in work, again where allowed by decree.[209]

---

204 art. L.3121-8 C. trav.
205 art. L.3121-8 C. trav.
206 art. L.3121-9 C. trav.
207 art. L.3121-16 C. trav.
208 art. L.3162-3 C. trav.
209 art. L.3131 C. trav.

Authorisation for daily maximum working hours – *Durée journalière maximale de travail*

The daily limit (*durée journalière maximale*) of working hours should not exceed 10 hours unless the *inspecteur du travail* (work inspector) has authorised it in circumstances fixed by decree, or in urgent circumstances (fixed by decree) or unless provided for to the contrary by a *une convention* or *accord d'entreprise* or *d'établissement* or, if none, by *convention* or *accord de branche* for reasons related to the organisation of the business with an overall limit of 12 hours per day.[210]

People under 18 may usually not work more than 8 hours per day although an additional 5 hours per week may be allowed after obtaining consent from the *inspecteur du travail* after obtaining a positive opinion from the work doctor. This must not exceed the daily or weekly limits that would be applicable to an adult.[211]

Maximum weekly limit – *Durée hebdomadaire maximale*

The weekly overall limit (*durée hebdomadaire maximale*) may not exceed 48 hours,[212] which is an "absolute maximum" (*durée maximale absolue*). This may be exceeded with the consent of the administrative authority in certain limited circumstances set out by decree, subject to an overall maximum of 60 hours per week. The *CSE* should forward its opinion on any demands for such authorisation to the *agent de contrôle de l'inspection du travail*.[213]

For employees working full time the normal limit is 35 hours per week[214] (working for less than 35 hours per week will usually be classified as part-time work).

The hours should also not exceed an average of 44 hours over a consecutive 12-week period.[215] That is a maximum average (*durée maximale moyenne*). A *convention, accord d'entreprise* or *d'établissement*, or if none a *convention* or *accord de branche* may exceed this subject to an overall limit of 46 hours over the 12 weeks.[216] There are additional exceptional circumstances where the 46 hours may be exceeded set out by decree of the *Conseil d'État*.

People under 18 may usually not work more than 35 hours per week, although an additional 5 hours per week may be allowed with the permission of the *inspecteur du travail* after obtaining a positive opinion from the work doctor. This must not exceed the daily or weekly limits that would be applicable to an adult.[217]

Consultation prior to making decisions, and notifications of decisions

---

210 art. L.3121-18-19 C. trav.
211 art. L.3162-1 C. trav.
212 art. L.3121-20 C. trav.
213 art. L.3121-21 C. trav.
214 art. L.3121-27 C. trav.
215 art. L.3121-22 C. trav.
216 art. L.3121-23 C. trav.
217 art. L.3162-1 C. trav.

to relevant authorities, shall be carried out in accordance with the rules applicable in each situation.

B) Supplementary hours – *Heures supplémentaires*

These are the hours worked at the request of the employer above the hours set by law or by *convention*. These are to be distinguished from *heures complémentaires* (complementary hours) which are those worked by a part-time worker in excess of their contractual hours. There is a separate section dealing with these below.

The usual working week is 35 hours for full-time employees.[218] Hours worked in excess of this will usually be *heures supplémentaires*.

Heures supplémentaires will be paid by an increase in salary (*majoration de salaire*) or in certain cases by compensatory breaks/leave (*un repos compensateur*).[219]

An employee who refuses to carry out supplementary hours may be subject to penalties including dismissal (unless the employer has not paid for previous supplementary hours).

In default of any applicable *accord* or *convention* then the *contingent annuel d'heures supplémentaires* is usually set at 220 hours.[220]

The rate of the additional remuneration or *contrepartie* may be set by an *accord de branche étendu* or an *accord d'entreprise ou d'établissement*.

The rate of increase of hourly rate may usually not be less than 10%.[221] In the absence of agreement to the contrary, the rates of hourly increase are usually set as follows:[222]

- The first additional 8 hours: +25%
- Over additional 8 hours: +50%.

The minimums at which the *contrepartie* (recompense, in this case in the form of rest time) may be set are the following,[223] which also apply where no agreement is reached:[224]

- Up to 20 employees: 50% of the additional hours over the annual contingent
- 20 employees upwards: 100%.

---

218 art. L.3121-27 C. trav.
219 art. L.3121-28 C. trav.
220 art. D.3121-24 C. trav.
221 art. L.3121-33 C. trav.
222 art. L.3121-36 C. trav.
223 art. L.3121-33 C. trav.
224 art. L.3121-38 C. trav.

C) Part-time work – *Travail à temps partiel*

Work is generally considered to be part time if a contract is for less than the *durée légale* (e.g. 35 hours per week) or the usual *durée* fixed by a *convention* or the usual in the establishment if that is less. This may be done by weekly, monthly or annual reference.[225]

Such employees have broadly speaking the same rights as full-time employees.[226]

Part-time employees will be given a minimum number of working hours. This may be fixed by a *convention* or *accord de branche étendu*[227] but where there is no such agreement the minimum will be 24 hours per week or the monthly equivalent or the equivalent calculated over the period chosen by a relevant *accord collectif*.[228]

Where the hours fixed by the *accord* are lower than the default minimum, certain additional protections are given to the employee.

Contracts may be made for work sharing a role. The contract must comply with the usual rules as if it was for 1 person in that role.

D) Other contracts that are not full time

There is provision for other types of contract that are not full time, such as those for intermittent work (*contrats de travail intermittent*), which will usually be a *CDI* and the use of which is quite restricted, and seasonal work (*contrats de travail saisonnier*), which will usually be either a *CDD* or a *CTT*.

E) Additional hours – *Heures complémentaires*

Heures complémentaires (additional hours) are those worked by a part-time worker in excess of their contractual hours. Additional hours must not raise the total of the hours worked by the part-time worker to the usual *durée légale* for a full-time employee as set by the usual laws/norms or if lower by *convention*.[229] Where the amount of hours worked reaches the usual working week of 35 hours, the employee may become entitled to apply to the *conseillers prud'homaux* for the contract to be re-classified as a full-time contract.

It is neither a *faute* nor a motive for dismissal for an employee to refuse

225 art. L.3123-1 C. trav.
226 art. L.3123-5 C. trav.
227 art. L.3123-19 C. trav.
228 art. L.3123-27 C. trav.
229 art. L.3123-9 C. trav.

to work *heures complémentaires* that are in excess of those provided for by the contract. It will also not be within the contractually provided limits if less than 3 days' notice of the *heures complémentaires* is provided by the employer.[230]

There are further limits to the amount of *heures complémentaires* that may be requested. Where there is *convention* or *accord d'entreprise* or *d'établissement*, or if none a *convention* or *accorde de branche étendu* the limit of the hours may not be above one-third of the weekly or monthly length of the contractual hours and where applicable calculated over the period chosen by a relevant *accord collectif*.[231]

Where no such agreement has been entered into, the number of hours required over a week, or a month, or any other period set out in an *accord collectif* may not exceed one-tenth of the weekly or monthly *durée de travail* in the contract and where applicable calculated over the period chosen by a relevant *accord collectif*.[232]

Employees must be paid for the additional hours worked at a rate higher than their usual hourly rate (which may be set by a *convention* or an *accord de branche étendu*) and this will usually be at least 10% more. Where there is no *convention* or an *accord de branche étendu* fixing a rate, then the minima will be 10% for each additional hour worked up to one-tenth of those provided for by the contract, and 25% for each hour between the tenth and a third of the hours provided for by the contract.[233]

---

230 art. L.3123-10 C. trav.
231 art. L.3123-20 C. trav.
232 art. L.3123-28 C. trav.
233 art. L.3123- 8, L.3123-21 et L.3123-29 C. trav.

14. Organisation of periods of variable work time (*Aménagement du temps de travail*) over a work period greater than a week

There are specific provisions allowing for arrangements for variable hours of work to be organised across different periods, and for the general rules to be adjusted within limits by collective arrangements or in some cases individual ones.

In such cases, additional hours worked that fall within the new variable hour scheme will not usually be classified as *heures supplémentaires*.

Where the variable hours are to be for a period of greater than a week, the period may not exceed 3 years where there is an *accord collectif* and 9 weeks where the organisation is made unilaterally by the employer. Where the period for calculation is 1 year, all hours over 1,607 hours will be *heures supplémentaires*. Whether the period is less or greater than 1 year, all hours above a weekly average of 35 hours will be *heures supplémentaires*.[234]

Where the reference period is greater than 1 week, employees are entitled to reasonable notice of any changes.[235]

The employer is subject to certain rules when an arrangement over several weeks is made unilaterally by them rather than by *accord*. In circumstances set by decree, where there are fewer than 50 employees, the arrangement may not exceed 9 weeks, and where there are more than 50, the arrangement may not exceed 4 weeks[236] unless it is a business that works continuously, in which case these limits do not apply.[237]

For certain individuals, it is possible for them to request and the business to organise a personal working hours arrangement (*horaire individualisé*, as opposed to the *horaire collectif de travail*, which is that which is uniform for all the employees). Depending upon the situation this may involve carrying hours from one week to another, or a period of flexible working time, and the

---

234 art. L.3121-41 C. trav.
235 art. L.3121-42 C. trav.
236 art. L.3121-45 C. trav.
237 art. L.3121-46 C. trav.

confirmatory advice of the *CSE* may be needed in some cases. Where there is no representative of the employees, the *inspecteur du travail* may in some cases apply an arrangement.[238]

A) Daily rest – *Repos quotidien*

The usual rule is that all employees are entitled to a consecutive rest period of at least 11 hours per day with exceptions in urgent situations or conditions set out in decrees.[239] This may be adjusted in certain circumstances by the employer by a *convention* or *accord d'entreprise* or *d'établissement* or if none a *convention* or *accord de branche*, for example where continuity of service is required.[240] An *accord collectif de travail* may not reduce the rest period below 9 hours.[241]

Young workers (*jeunes travailleurs*, defined as being at least 15 years old and less than 18) have a longer entitlement of 12 hours, and 14 if they are less than 16 years old.[242]

No daily work period may continue for 6 hours without the employee having a break of at least 20 minutes, but a *convention* or an *accord d'entreprise* or *d'établissement* or in default a *convention* or *accord de branche* may set a longer rest period.[243]

Jeunes travailleurs are entitled to a break of 30 minutes after working for 4 and a half hours.[244]

In circumstances where the rest periods are reduced, the employee must be compensated for the lost rest time, which may in some circumstances be either financial or by compensatory rest hours.

B) Weekly rest time – *Repos hebdomadaire*

Employees in general have a right to 1 continuous day (a period of 24 hours) off per week[245] (*repos hebdomadaire* – weekly rest). This will usually be Sunday,[246] however there are possible derogations to the choice of day, e.g. where production, the activity or the public require it;[247] in the food

---

238 art. L.3121-48 et L.3121-49 C. trav.
239 art. L.3131-1 C. trav.
240 art. L.3131-2 C. trav.
241 art. D.3131-6 C. trav.
242 art. L.3164-1 C. trav.
243 art. L.3121-16 and art. L.3121-17 C. trav.
244 art. L.3162-3 C. trav.
245 art. L.3132-1 and art. L.3132-2 C. trav.
246 art. L.3132-3 C. trav.
247 art. L.3132-12 C. trav.

business;[248] in industries or industrial enterprises where provided for by *une convention* or an *accord d'entreprise* or *d'établissement* or if none by a *convention* or *accord d'entreprise* or, where none, in some cases by the *inspecteur du travail* after consultation with the *CSE* if it exists; derogations granted by the *préfet* or *maire*; and derogations granted due to particular geographical issues.[249]

There are various exceptions to the usual rule of 24 hours' rest and how it is dealt with, e.g. in relation to:

- urgent work[250]

- industries dealing with perishable matters or having to deal with an exceptional increase in work[251]

- work in ports, landing stages and similar[252]

- seasonal activity[253]

- work involving cleaning of industrial places and maintenance[254]

- national defence[255]

- businesses that work continuously[256]

- guards and concierges for business and industrial premises.[257]

The *Code du travail* sets out some circumstances where mandatory compensation must be paid to people working on Sunday. Compensation may also be agreed by *conventions* or by *accords collectifs* applicable to the enterprise, or may be agreed in the employment contract itself.

Jeunes travailleurs are usually entitled to 2 continuous days' rest per week, and where collective arrangements seek to change this, the rest may still usually not be reduced below 36 consecutive hours.[258]

---

248 art. L.3132-13 C. trav.
249 arts. L.3132-14 à L.3132-27 C. trav.
250 art. L.3132-4 C. trav.
251 art. L.3132-5 C. trav.
252 art. L.3132-6 C. trav.
253 art. L.3132-7 C. trav.
254 art. L.3132-8 C. trav.
255 art. L.3132-9 C. trav.
256 art. L.3132-10 C. trav.
257 art. L.3132-11 C. trav.
258 art. L.3164 C. trav.

C) Collective agreements for allocated amounts of working time

A *convention de forfait* (collective agreement for allocated amounts of working time) may be agreed in hours on a weekly, monthly or annual basis; a *forfait* in days may be agreed on an annual basis.[259] It must be agreed by the employee and be in writing.[260]

Annual *forfaits* for hours or days may be made by an *accord collectif d'entreprise ou d'établissement* or in default, by *une convention* or an *accord de branche*, in which case the relevant procedures must be followed.[261]

For annual *forfaits* for hours or for days, the number of working days set by any collective agreement may not be more than 218[262] and there are rules limiting the total worked even where an employee renounces rest days.[263]

Forfait in hours per week or per month
1) possible for all employees[264]

2) remuneration proposed must be at least equal to the minimum remuneration applicable in the enterprise for the number of hours corresponding to the *forfait* plus any relevant increases for supplementary hours[265]

Forfait in hours per annum
1) possible for *cadres* whose functions involve them not conforming to the collective hours and for employees benefitting from a real autonomy in the organisation of their working their working time[266]

2) remuneration proposed must be at least equal to the minimum remuneration applicable in the enterprise for the number of hours corresponding to the *forfait* plus any relevant increases for supplementary hours[267]

---

259 art. L.3121-54 C. trav.
260 art. L.3121-55 C. trav.
261 art. L.3121-63 C. trav.
262 art. L.3121-64 C. trav.
263 art. L.3121-66 C. trav.
264 art. L.3121-56 C. trav.
265 art. L.3121-57 C. trav.
266 art. L.3121-56 C. trav.
267 art. L.3121-57 C. trav.

Forfait **in days per annum**

1) possible for *cadres* who have a real autonomy in the organisation of their time and whose functions do not require them to follow the collective hours; and for employees for whom the length of time cannot be predetermined and who have a real autonomy in the organisation of their time[268]

2) employees who have entered into a *forfait-jours* are not subject to the usual rules concerning working time[269]

3) The employer must regularly check that the workload is reasonable and allows a good division of the work time[270]

4) There is express provision for an employee who receives remuneration manifestly not sufficient with regard to the constraints of the work to make an application to seek an indemnity for the prejudice caused taking into account the employee's level in the business and their qualifications, notwithstanding contractual or *conventionnelle* clauses[271]

5) An employee who wishes to may renounce part of their rest days in return for an increase in their remuneration. The increase should not be less than 10%. Such an agreement may only last for its current year and any renewal must be express.[272]

---

268 art. L.3121-58 C. trav.
269 art. L.3121-62 C. trav.
270 art. L.3121-60 C. trav.
271 art. L.3121-61 C. trav.
272 art. L.3121-59 C. trav.

15. Holidays/leave – *Congés*

The length of the paid leave (*congés payés*) is calculated by reference to the worked days carried out during the reference period (*une période de référence*).

The basic rule is that any employee has the right to 2 and a half working days' (paid) leave per month of work up to 30 days.[273] Where the number of days leave is less than a whole number, the number is rounded up to the next full day.[274]

Employees who are aged under 21 years on 30 April of the preceding year are entitled to 2 additional days of holiday per child (living in their household, under 15 years old or disabled) but this is reduced to 1 day where the holiday entitlement is no greater than 6 days.

Employees aged 21 or older at that date are also entitled to 2 additional days per child but in this case the reduction above does not apply and the total days of *congés* should not exceed 30 days.[275]

The working days (*jours ouvrables*) are calculated using all the days of the week except the day of rest and any bank holidays given by the enterprise.

Part-time employees have the same rights as full-time employees.

A) Organisation of paid leave

The period for which the employees have the right to take their leave should usually include the period from 1 May to 31 October.[276] However, the organisation of the period for the holidays and how they are allocated within that time may be set by an *accord d'entreprise* or *d'établissment*, or if none a *convention* or *accord de branche* or in the absence of such agreements by the employer after consultation with the *CSE*.[277]

Taking paid leave is allowed in principle from the moment of the commencement of employment.[278]

The usual rule is that continuous leave (usually this will be the *congé*

---

273 art. L.3141-3 C. trav.
274 art. L.3141-7 C. trav.
275 art. L.3141-8 C. trav.
276 art. L.3141-13 C. trav.
277 art. L.3141-16 C. trav.
278 art. L.3141-12 C. trav.

principal – main holiday) should be no more than 24 working days (four weeks) but this does not need to apply where there are particular geographical constraints, or the employee lives in a household with a handicapped adult or child or an elderly person or one with limited autonomy.[279]

Where the *congés* are for not more than 12 days, the employee is entitled to take the time as one continuous period.[280] With regard to days of holiday above those 12, then, unless an agreement with the employee sets out otherwise, employees will be entitled to additional days of *congés* if holiday is allocated outside the period 1 May to 31 October as follows:[281]

3 to 5 days outside that period – an additional 1 day
6 or more days outside that period – 2 additional days

Where the entitlement to *congés* is for over 12 days, if the employer wishes to divide up the entitlement into shorter periods, then the consent of the employee is required unless the time off falls within a period when the establishment is closed. At least 1 of the periods taken off should still be at least 12 continuous days.[282]

An *accord* or *convention* may in certain circumstances agree that days may be carried over up to 31 December of the year following the reference period, and it may set the conditions.[283]

B) Payment for leave

Holiday pay is known as *une indemnité de congés payés*. There are set rules for the calculation of this, the basic starting point being a payment of one-tenth of the gross remuneration received by the employee over the reference period and it also should not be less than what the employee would have received if they had not been on holiday then.[284]

If the contract is terminated, the employer must pay the employee in lieu of any untaken leave (*une indemnité compensatrice*) that has been accrued.[285]

It is usually possible for the contract or a collective agreement to provide for payments higher than the normal minima.

---

279 art. L.3141-17 C. trav.
280 art. L.3141-18 C. trav.
281 art. L.3141-23 C. trav.
282 art. L.3141-19 C. trav.
283 art. L.3141-22 C. trav.
284 art. L.3141-24 C. trav.
285 art. L.3141-28 C. trav.

C) Leave for family events

Certain family events such as maternity, adoption, marriage etc. entitle the employee to additional leave related to that event. Examples are set out below. There is not always an entitlement to salary for the leave but benefits may be paid by the State. It is usually possible for contracts or collective agreements to provide for longer leave.

Maternity leave – *Congé de maternité*	Unpaid – varies[286] depending on various matters including the number of prior children, plus the number in the birth (e.g. twins) – minimum at 16 weeks – paid by the social security system on a daily rate
Adoption leave – *Congé d'adoption*	Unpaid – varies, starting from 10 weeks for a single child,[287] paid by the social security system at a daily rate. Applies also to cohabiting partners.
Paternity leave – *Congé de paternité*	Unpaid – cannot be taken in parts, 11 consecutive calendar days for the birth of a child, 18 if multiple birth,[288] paid by the social security system at a daily rate. May be taken cumulatively with the holiday of 3 days given for the birth of the child. Applies also to cohabiting partners.
Marriage leave or for entering into a *PACS* – *Congé lié au mariage du salarié/pour la conclusion d'un pacte civile de solidarité*	Paid – 4 days[289]
Holiday leave for the marriage of a child – *Congé lié au mariage d'un enfant*	Paid – 1 day[290]
Parental leave related to the birth or adoption of a child – *Congé lié à la naissance ou à l'adoption d'un enfant*	Paid – 3 days[291]

---

286 art. L.1225-17, 1225-18, L.1225-19 C. trav.
287 art. L.1225-37 C. trav.
288 art. L.1225-35 C. trav.
289 art. L.3142-4 C. trav.
290 art. L.3142-4 C. trav.
291 art. L.3142-4 C. trav.

Death of a child	Paid – 5 day[292]
Leave related to the death of a spouse,civil partner, father, mother, father-in-law or mother-in-law, brother, sister, of the employee – *Congé lié au décès du conjoint, partenaire lié par un PACS, père, de la mere, du beau-père, de la belle-mère, d'un frère, d'une soeur, du salarié*	Paid – 3 days[293]
Leave for a sick or injured child – *Congé pour un enfant malade ou accidenté*	Unpaid – 3 days per year, 5 if the child is under one year old or if the employee is responsible for three or more children aged under 16[294]

D) Other leave

Employees can take unpaid leave for certain purposes. This entitlement is usually related to the length of service of the employee. Examples are given below, with examples of some of the conditions applicable (the conditions given. It is usually possible for the rights to be varied by contract or collective agreement, but not if that reduces the employee's basic rights as set out in the *Code du travail*.

Leave	Some of the usual conditions	Usual length
Sabbatical *congé sabbatique*	1) Employee worked in that enterprise for at least 36 months (consecutive or not) 2) Employee been working for at least 6 years 3) The employer can in certain circumstances contest the holiday or defer it	6 months minimum, 11 months maximum[295]
"Parental education" leave *congé d'éducation parentale*	1) Employed for 1 year 2) Can be for leave, or to work part time but not less than 16 hours per week[296]	Varies depending upon the number of children, starting from 1 year, may be renewed twice[297]

292 art. L.3142-4 C. trav.
293 art. L.3142-4 C. trav.
294 art. L.1225-61 C. trav.
295 art. L.3142-34 C. trav.
296 art. L.1225-47 C. trav.
297 art. L.1225-48 C. trav.

Leave to set up a business *congé pour création d'entreprise*	1) At least 24 months' employment in that enterprise, consecutive or not[298] 2) Can be for leave, or to work part time 3) The employer may in certain circumstances contest the leave or defer it	1 year, renewable once[299]

---

298 art. L.3142-119 C. trav
299 art. L.3142-119 C. trav.

16. Bank holidays – *Jours fériés*; and solidarity day – *la journée de solidarité*

A *jour férié* is a bank holiday; not all bank holidays in France are days off (*chômé*). Where the employees do not have to work they are usually (not always) paid. Collective agreements may adjust which of the dates are worked, and in the absence of a collective agreement this will usually be set by the employer. There are 11 in France currently, which are listed in the *Code du travail*:[300]

1 January
Easter Monday (*lundi de Pâques*)
1 May (*fête du travail* – fête of work)
8 May (*Victoire* 1945)
Ascension Thursday
Pentecostal Monday
14 July (*fête nationale* – national fête)
15 August (Assumption)
All Saints (*Toussaint*)
11 November (Armistice 1918)
Christmas Day

Only 1 May is mandatorily both *férié* and *chômé*.[301] If the employee is in employment where the day cannot be taken off and the employee works on 1 May, they must be paid double their usual remuneration.[302]

For other bank holidays, in the absence of an agreement by contract or *convention* the contrary, the employee does not have any automatic right to anything other than ordinary pay.

Generally speaking, people under the age of 18 should not work on *jours fériés*.[303] In certain regulated circumstances they may be allowed to, but usually only in cases where they will then be entitled to 36 hours consecutively off

---

300 art. L.3133-1 C. trav.
301 art. L.3133-4 C. trav.
302 art. L.3133-6 C. trav.
303 art. L.3164-6 C. trav.

(this may apply for example in industries that work continuously).[304]

If the day is *chômé*, employees employed there for at least 3 months who work the bank holiday will be entitled to pay (this does not apply to those working from home, nor to intermittent or temporary workers; for seasonal workers, separate work periods may be cumulated to achieve the 3 months).[305]

There is no automatic entitlement to bridging days where a *jour férié* falls 1 day or 2 away from the weekly day(s) off. Nevertheless, such days off (known as *ponts*) are commonly taken in France and may be the subject of the contract, *accord* etc.

A) Day of solidarity – *La journée de solidarité* [306]

This is a 7-hour day the purpose of which is to provide money for actions benefitting old people and disabled people. Employees are obliged to carry out 1 additional day per year of normally paid work of 7 hours, which is unpaid. The employer must pay a sum to the State. For part-time workers the time will be calculated pro-rata.

The procedures for the day of solidarity may be set out in an *accord d'entreprise* or *d'établissment* or in default by a *convention* or an *accord de branche*.[307] The agreement may fix the day of solidarity on a bank holiday (applicable ones other than 1 May) or to reduce the *RTT* (*réduction de temps de travail* – reduction of work time, i.e. the days allowed off work) by 1 day, or by any other method leading to the working of the seven hours usually not worked.

In default of any form of collective agreement, the procedures will be set by the employer after consultation with the *CSE*.[308]

Usually where an employee has already worked a solidarity day with a previous employer in the same year, they are entitled to payment and time off for any new solidarity day that they are asked to work. The employee may also refuse to work the day in this case, and the refusal shall not be a *faute* or reason for dismissal.[309]

---

304 art. L.3164-7 C. trav.
305 art. L.3133-3 C. trav.
306 art. L.3133-7 to art. L.3133-10 C. trav.
307 art. L.3133-11 C. trav.
308 art. L.3133-12 C. trav.
309 art. L.3133-10 C. trav.

B) Holiday account – *Le compte épargne-temps (CET)*

This may be set up by a *convention* or an *accord d'entreprise* or *d'établissement* or, if none, by *convention* or *accord de branche*.[310] The conditions and procedures will be set out in the agreement.

This scheme allows the employee to accumulate in a fund their rights to paid leave or to have remuneration in lieu of a period of leave or rest not taken, or money due in relation to it. Only days of holiday entitlement lasting in excess of 24 *jours ouvrables* of entitlement may be saved in the account.[311]

C) Record of voluntary work – *Compte d'engagement citoyen*

A formal record may be kept of certain voluntary or charitable work that may then be used to count towards professional development/training or holiday days for those purposes.[312]

---

310 art. L.3151-1 C. trav.
311 art. L.3151-2 C. trav.
312 art. L.5151-7 C. trav.

17. Professional development – *La formation professionnelle*

The employer must ensure that the employee is suited to their job *(l'adaptation des salaries à leur poste de travail)*. The employer must also ensure the ongoing capability of the employee to do their job *(maintien de leur capacité à occupier leur poste de travail)*, for example with regard to changing technology.[313] Time spent training which is intended to ensure that the employee can do their job or adapt to the evolution of their work as provided for by their contract counts as working time and should be remunerated as such.[314]

Employers should allocate a provision each year for the funding of training. The basic minimum amount is normally set by rules, which may depend for example on the number of employees.[315]

As a general rule, the employee may not refuse valid training otherwise they may face disciplinary action, which could include dismissal.

Training may within limits be carried out outside the legal working hours or those provided for by *convention* if there is an agreement to this effect between the employee and employer.[316] It will not be either a *faute* or a potential reason for dismissal if the employee refuses to do training outside working hours.[317]

A) Training plan – *Plan de formation*

This includes all training that the employer decides that the employees will undertake.

Every 2 years the employer should have a meeting with the employee to assess their professional development in terms of training. Every 6 years the employer should have a meeting providing an overall summary and statement of the situation.[318]

---

313 art. L.6321-1 C. trav.
314 art. L.6321-2 C. trav.
315 art. R.6331 C. trav.
316 art. L.6321-6 C. trav.
317 art. L.6321-7 C. trav.
318 art. L.6315-1 C. trav.

B) Individual training account – *Compte personnel de formation*

This is an account that an employee or a person seeking work may open. It is a formal record that allows them to accumulate an entitlement to hours of training as a result of hours of work completed. Every employee (including e.g. in *professions libérales*) is entitled to create such an account but it is not mandatory.[319] The account can be transferred by the employee from one employer to another.[320]

The employer will usually pay for the training, but it may also be paid for by the employee, by relevant associations or even by the State.[321] The employee should continue to receive their usual remuneration during the training period.[322]

There are set calculations for how the entitlement is made to give basic normal levels. In general the account entitlement is for 24 hours per year of full-time work, until the total accumulated over the years reaches 120 hours. After that point, the entitlement is 12 hours per complete year worked up to a total of 150.[323] There are certain groups of workers who will usually have a greater entitlement, e.g. those with certain listed lower levels of current qualification.[324]

The employee may propose training. There are rules that set out the usual types of relevant training that qualify.

The basic rules may generally be augmented by contract or collective agreement.

C) Personal leave for training – *Le congé individuel de formation (CIF)*

The purpose of this arrangement is to allow employees to choose other training for themselves, independently of that available under the business's arrangements.[325] The basic rules and rights may be augmented by the contract or by collective agreements.

This further training may be carried out partly or wholly during or outside working hours.[326]

---

319 art. L.6323-2 C. trav.
320 art. L.6323-3 C. trav.
321 art. L.6323-4 C. trav.
322 art. L.6323-18 C. trav.
323 art. L.6323-11 C. trav.
324 art. L.6323-11-1 C. trav.
325 art. L.6322-1 C. trav.
326 art. L.6322-2 C. trav.

The employee must usually have been in their job for a minimum length of time, which will be set by *décret*.[327] The employer has certain rights to defer any such training, and this will depend on matters such as the number of employees in the business.

In general the leave may last a maximum of 1 year if it is full time, or 1,200 hours if part time.[328]

Provided relevant conditions are fulfilled and procedures followed, the employee will be entitled to a certain remuneration for this leave, which will usually be paid by the employer but reimbursed to them by the State.[329] The remuneration will usually be set by *décret* and may be less than the usual salary of the employee when they are working.[330] Higher remuneration may be arranged by agreement.

D) Validation of experience – *Validation des aquis de l'expérience*

It is possible to apply to have certain types of relevant experience officially recognised so that they will count towards certain types of diploma and other work qualifications.[331]

E) Various other rights to time off for professional development

Various other rights exist to allow employees and those in search of work time for relevant matters, e.g. to take exams, or for research.

---

327 art. L.6322-4 C. trav.
328 art. L.6322-12 C. trav.
329 art. L.6322-20 C. trav.
330 art. L.6322-17 C. trav.
331 art. L.6411-1 C. trav.

18. Internal rules and regulations – *Le règlement intérieur*

The employer has authority/power to make the rules/regulations within the enterprise; this is the *pouvoir réglementaire*. The employees must respect those rules and regulations during their work there. This flows from the position of "subordination" of the employee.

The rule book (the *règlement intérieur*) should also set out relevant provisions relating to the health and safety systems and conditions under which employees may be called on to participate in the re-establishment of the health and safety conditions when they have been compromised. It must deal with disciplinary action (*sanctions disciplinaires*).[332] It must set out the procedures to be followed in cases of sexual harassment (*harcèlement sexuel*) or bullying (*harcèlement moral*).[333]

The rule book may not interfere with the rights of people or with personal and group freedoms, and restrictions must not be excessive and must be justified by the nature of the task to be carried out, and proportionate to the aim sought.[334] It must not be discriminatory.[335]

Where an enterprise has fewer than 20 employees there is no obligation to have a rule book.

Where an enterprise habitually has at least 20 employees it must create a rule book;[336] failure to do so renders the enterprise liable to a fine, which may be up to 750 euros.[337]

The rule book must be in writing, in French (although it may also be accompanied by copies in other languages as well)[338] and must show the date that it came into force.[339] It must be brought to the attention of the employees and to all people having access to the work places (usually at least by notices put up within the enterprise).[340]

---

332 art. L.1321-1 C. trav.
333 art. L.1321-2 C. trav.
334 art. L.1121-1 C. trav.
335 art. L.1132-1 C. trav.
336 art. L.1311-2 C. trav.
337 art. R.1323-1 C. trav.
338 art. L.1321-6 C. trav.
339 art. L.1321-4 C. trav.
340 art. R.1321-1 C. trav.

Prior to its coming into effect the employer must seek the opinion of the *CSE*.[341] The rule book, together with a copy of the opinions of the above, must be delivered to the work inspector and a copy of the *règlement* deposited with the clerk (*greffe*) of the *conseil de prud'hommes*.[342] The same formalities apply to any subsequent modification.

A) Control of the rule book

There are many regulations and rules that control the restrictions and procedures that may be used. There is also provision for monitoring of the book by external authority and for modification where considered necessary.

At all times the work inspector may require the removal or modification of any part of the rule book which does not comply with law, or may require additions where appropriate.[343] To do this the inspector must deliver a reasoned notification of their decision to the employer and also for information to the members of the *CSE*.[344] There are procedures for appealing the decision to the *directeur régional des entreprises, de la concurrence, de la consommation, du travail et de l'emploi* (the regional director of business, competition, consumption, work and employment) within 2 months following notification of the decision to the works inspector.[345]

In the event of a court action, the *conseil des prud'hommes* may remove any rule or regulation from the rule book that is contrary to the relevant laws and other legal requirements.

---

341 art. L.1321-4 C. trav.
342 art. R.1321-2 C. trav.
343 art. L.1322-1 C. trav.
344 art. L.1322-2 C. trav.
345 art. R.1322-1 C. trav.

19. Employer's disciplinary rights – *Pouvoir disciplinaire*

A disciplinary power flows from the subordinate position of the employees, however the law controls the limits and use of the power and related procedures.

The internal disciplinary rules will apply, as well as those in any collective agreement, statutes of personnel of public enterprises, internal rules, as well as the right to have the matter put to a *conseil de discipline* (disciplinary panel) where applicable.

Generally speaking, whether the behaviour of the employee constitutes an action that may be subject to disciplinary proceedings is to be determined by the employer. A disciplinable action or omission will be one that does not correspond to the normal execution of the work contract.

A) Disciplinary offences – *La faute disciplinaire*

There are various terms that may be used to classify degrees of seriousness of offence:

faute légère – minor offence; may be subject to disciplinary action not including dismissal

faute simple – this type of offence may still lead to dismissal even though it is not sufficiently serious to be classified as *faute grave* or *lourde*. This might be a mistake, or negligence

faute sérieuse – serious offence; may lead to dismissal if the employee is employed on a *CDI* and the behaviour is prejudicial to the enterprise

faute grave – an offence so serious that the employment relationship cannot be maintained; the employee loses their right to dismissal payments (apart from *indemnité de congés payés*)

faute lourde – the most serious category of offence, indicating behaviour on the part of the employee with intention to terminate the contract.

There is a limitation period for the employer to take disciplinary action against facts that are at fault (*prescription des faits fautifs*): no disciplinary action may be carried out if 2 months have elapsed from the day when the employer became aware of the truth, the nature and the extent of the facts.[346]

B) Disciplinary penalties – *Sanctions disciplinaires*

Under the *Code du travail*, disciplinary sanctions include all measures taken, other than verbal observations, by the employer following an action deemed to be a disciplinary matter.[347]

Fines and other financial penalties are not allowed,[348] and the sanctions must not be or be used in a manner that is discriminatory.[349]

A double sanction may not be imposed for the same offence.[350] Where the prior sanction occurred over 3 years ago from the beginning of the new disciplinary action, it may not be taken into account (in general there is a limitation period for sanctions – *prescription des sanctions disciplinaires*).[351]

The rule book must set out the sanctions that apply in the enterprise and also classify them by order of gravity. The French terms used, in order of seriousness (the scale of sanctions – *l'échelle des sanctions*), are:

l'avertissment – warning
le blâme – reprimand
la mise à pied disciplinaire – suspension
la mutation – transfer
la rétrogradation – demotion
le licenciement – dismissal.

C) The disciplinary procedure – *Procédure disciplinaire*

Where the alleged facts are sufficiently serious, it is possible for an employee to be immediately asked to leave their work, however no final decision may be made unless and until the formal procedures have been followed.[352]

Where a sanction decided upon is not dismissal, the employee has the right to contest the disciplinary action by bringing the case before the *conseil de prud'hommes*. The *conseil* has the power to revoke the disciplinary action if it is deemed irregular, unjustified or disproportionate.[353] It may order damages and interest to be paid.

---

346 art. L.1332-4 C. trav.
347 art. L.1331-1 C. trav.
348 art. L.1331-2 C. trav.
349 art. L.1132-1 C. trav.
350 the rule of non bis in idem – not twice for the same thing, i.e. double jeopardy
351 art. L.1332-5 C. trav.
352 art. L.1332-3 C. trav.
353 art. L.1333-2 C. trav.

There are additional procedures and other court proceedings applicable in relation to potential dismissals/decisions to dismiss which are discussed in the section relating to dismissals.

The procedure should vary according to the gravity of the sanction.

Minor sanction –
one which does not stop the employee being present in the enterprise, their role or their career (e.g. notice, warning, *rappel à l'ordre or lettre d'observation*)

No interview required prior to penalty. The employer must notify the employee in writing of the accusations against him by signed-for letter with acknowledgment of receipt *(LRAR - lettre recommandé avec accusé de réception)* or by having it delivered to them in person and signed for.[354]

More serious sanction –
one which will have either an immediate or subsequent effect on the presence of the employee in the enterprise, on their role, their career or their salary

1) The employer must notify the employee in writing of the accusations against him by signed – for letter with acknowledgment of receipt *LRAR (lettre recommandé avec accusé de réception)* or by having it delivered to them in person and signed for.[355]

Where the employer is considering dismissal, the employee must be called *(la convocation)* to an interview *(entretien)* by this or another *LRAR*, which must state the purpose of the interview, the date, time and place of the meeting, and that the employee is entitled to be accompanied by a person of their choice from the business.[356] Where the employer is considering dismissal, the employee must also be notified in the letter that if there are no institutions representing the personnel in the business, the employee may be assisted either by a person they choose from the business, or by a counsellor from a list held by the administrative authority.[357]

2) At the meeting, the employer must set out the reason for the proposed disciplinary action, and the disciplinary action, and receive the explanations of the employee.[358]

3) The disciplinary action to be taken together with reasons must be put into effect (and then provided in writing to the employee) at least 2 *jours ouvrables* (working days) and no later than one month after the meeting.[359]

354 art. L.1332-1 C. trav.
355 art. L.1332-1 C. trav.
356 arts. L.1332-2 et R.1332-1 C. trav.
357 art. L.1232-4 C. trav.
358 art. L.1332-2 C. trav.
359 art. L.1332-2 C. trav.

20. Control of the use of the internet in the workplace and cyber surveillance

Article L.1121-1 of the *Code du travail* sets out that nothing may affect people's rights or affect personal or collective liberties unless it is justified by the nature of the job to be carried out and proportionate (the principle of *proportionalité*) to the intended outcome.

The employer must be transparent in the methods of control and secret surveillance is not allowed except inasmuch as it complies with the above.[360] The obligation to be transparent (transparency – *transparence*) involves informing the employees involved, and also informing and consulting the *CSE* before putting into action any such methods. Evidence collected in breach of the controls may not be used against the employee.[361]

Employees have a right to respect for their private lives, even during the course of working hours. This implies privacy of correspondence, including mail. The employer is not allowed to intrude on personal correspondence sent or received by electronic means using equipment provided for the employee's work, even where the employer has forbidden the use of the equipment for non-professional purposes.[362] This type of behaviour by the employer may be subject to possible serious criminal penalties including a fine of up to 45,000 euros or even a prison sentence of up to 1 year.[363]

The European Court of Human Rights has recently considered this area and confirmed limits on how an employee may be monitored in work.

Where an employer believes that the employee is breaching trust or confidentiality, the employer may seek authorisation from a judge to use a *huissier* (a type of qualified legal professional who deals with process-serving, debt recovery and enforcing judgments) to access the employee's personal emails.[364]

---

360 Soc. 20 nov. 1991
361 Soc. 4 juill. 2012
362 Soc. 2 oct. 2001
363 art. L.226-1 du Code pén.
364 Soc. 17 juin 2009

21. Discrimination – *La discrimination*

Direct and indirect discrimination is prohibited[365] in the recruitment process, in access to training courses or training periods within the enterprise, disciplinary procedures and penalties, dismissal or any other measure, remuneration, *reclassement*, particular use (*affection*), qualification, *classification*, promotion, transfer or renewal of contract by reason of:

background
age
sex
morals
sexual orientation
family situation
genetic characteristics
belonging (either real or supposed) to an ethnic group, a nation or a race
political opinions
union or mutualist activity
religious convictions
physical appearance
family name
health or handicap unless certified by a work doctor.

Direct discrimination (*discrimination directe*) occurs when a person is treated in a less favourable manner because of one of the subjective matters set out in the relevant article in the Code.

Indirect discrimination (*discrimination indirecte*) occurs when a criterium, apparently neutral but not objective, is used that may lead to a disadvantage for certain people in comparison with others.

The principle of non-discrimination (*le principe de non-discrimination*) does not always prohibit differences in treatment if that involves a business requirement where the objective is legal and the requirement is proportionate.

---

365 art. L.1132-1 C. trav. See also art. 225-1 C. pén.

A) Procedure

A victim of discrimination may bring an action before the *conseil de prud'hommes* and also the *inspection du travail*.

The victim may also bring the matter before the *Défenseur des droits* (Defender of Rights – an institution set up in the French constitution to oversee rights, to defend people where their rights may have been abused and to assist in enabling all to benefit from their rights) who may for example instigate an inquiry, organise mediation (*médiation*) or impose a criminal penalty.

There are certain circumstances in which the union may themselves bring proceedings with regard to perceived discrimination against employees or applicants for work.

B) Burden of proof – *La charge de la preuve*

The applicant to the court bringing an allegation must show the necessary facts which let it be supposed that there has been direct or indirect discrimination. Consequently the burden is on the defendant to prove that the decision was justified by elements involving no discrimination.[366] The judge may require provision of all further information that is necessary to make a decision.

C) Criminal penalties for discrimination

The employee may make a direct criminal complaint. Penalties for discrimination are set out in the *Code pénal* (Penal Code).[367] The employer risks becoming subject to a fine of up to 45,000 euros and a prison sentence of up to 3 years.

---

366 art. L.1134-1 C. trav.
367 art. 225-2 C. pén.

22. Sexual harassment and bullying – *Harcèlement sexuel* and *harcèlement moral*

A) Obligations of the employer and the employees' delegates

The employer must take all necessary steps to prevent sexual harassment and bullying.[368] The employer must where applicable punish the offender using the disciplinary code.

The delegates should exercise their right to draw matters to attention where there is sexual harassment or bullying.

The unions may bring legal proceedings against the offenders but only if they have the written consent of the victim.[369]

B) Sexual harassment

1) Definition

Sexual harassment occurs when there is unwanted repeated behaviour of a sexual nature with the intent of affecting the dignity of a person by being degrading or humiliating and/or creating an environment that is intimidating, hostile, or offensive. It also includes even 1 single serious act that pressurises the employee with a view to obtaining an act of a sexual nature either for the person carrying out the offence or for a third party.[370]

Thus, generally speaking, unless the behaviour is an attempt to obtain sexual acts, it will not be covered by this offence unless there is more than 1 incident;[371] however, only a short period of time of the behaviour is necessary to categorise it this way.[372]

---

368 art. L.1152-4 et art. L.1153-5 C. trav.
369 art. L.1154-2 C. trav.
370 art. L.1153-1 C. trav.
371 Soc. 14 nov. 2007
372 Soc. 26 mai 2010

2) Penalties

Action may be brought as a civil or a criminal action.

An employee who carries out behaviour of this nature is likely to be subject to disciplinary proceedings[373] and this may be classified as *faute grave*.[374]

On a civil basis, an employee may seek damages and interest for any *préjudice moral* (moral prejudice – e.g. hurt feelings, psychological damage, non-physical non-economic loss etc.) suffered. Any measure taken by the employer with regard to an employee who has refused to submit to sexual harassment will be null even where the harassment was not repeated.[375]

On a criminal basis, penalties including a fine of 3,750 euros and/or imprisonment for up to 1 year may be ordered, and also in some circumstances specified publications of the judgment at the expense of the party found guilty.[376]

3) Proof

The employee must establish the facts which lead to a presumption of sexual harassment. The defendant then has the burden of proving that the behaviour did not constitute sexual harassment.[377]

C) Bullying – Harcèlement moral

1) Definition

Bullying is defined as repeated behaviour (*agissements répétés*) where the object or effect is to alter the work conditions such that this change that may affect the rights and the dignity of the employee, alter their mental or physical health, or have a negative effect on their future career.[378]

2) Penalties and burden of proof

These are the same as for sexual harassment, including for the burden of proof.[379]

---

373 art. L.1153-6 C. trav.
374 Soc. 5 mars 2002
375 art. L.1153-2 C. trav.
376 art. L.1155-2 C. trav.
377 art. L.1154-1 C. trav.
378 art. L.1152-1 C. trav.
379 art. L.1154-1 C. trav.

23. Employees' representatives

There are various different forms of body representing employees. There are standard rules that will usually govern each of these, however there will in many cases be some room for adjustment by collective agreement or other contract, usually only as long as the basic minimum protection for employees is retained.

A) Very small, and small to medium-sized businesses[380]

In enterprises with up to 11 employees which have no union delegate, and in enterprises which have between 11 and 20 employees which have no elected member from the delegation of the *CSE*, the employer may put to referendum a plan for agreement on the topics that are eligible for negotiation in the enterprise.

Where there are up to 49 employees, in the absence of union delegates, the employer may negotiate with 1 or more employee(s) who are expressly mandated by 1 or more unions that are representative at national and inter-professional level, whether or not the employee is a member of the delegation of the *CSE*. The employer may also negotiate with 1 of the titular members of the personnel delegation of the *CSE*.

There are also provisions to enable similar negotiations in larger businesses.

B) Work union – *Syndicat professionnel*

Unions in France have their own civil legal status.[381] They are subject to rules regarding their set-up and use. To be authorised to negotiate *conventions* and *accords collectifs de travail* unions must be properly set up professional ones and must negotiate in accordance with the rules set out in the *Code du travail*.[382]

Employees have the right to join any work union of their choice and

---

380 art. L.2232-21 to 23 C. trav.
381 art. L.2132-1 C. trav.
382 art. L.2132-2 C. trav.

cannot be disciplined or dismissed for this or for participating in any union activity.[383] They are also entitled to leave any such union at any time.[384]

Unions are assessed with regard to their representativeness at various different levels: the basic criteria required include e.g. respect for republican values, independence, financial transparency, at least 2 years in the work field and geographical area related to the area of negotiation, audience achieved with regard to the area of negotiation, influence, number of members and subscriptions.[385] To be considered representative in a business or establishment it must also fulfil other criteria, including that it must have received at least 10% of the votes in the first rounds of the elections of the holders of the *CSE*.[386]

Once any union has more than 1 member in a business, a representative union complying with the relevant rules may set up a union section (*section syndicale*) in the business to ensure the representation of the material and personal wellbeing of its members.[387]

Once there are at least 200 employees in an establishment, the employer must provide a place for the union(s) to use. When there are at least 1,000 employees, the employer should provide to each *section syndicale* created by a representative union that is represented in the business or establishment a suitable area, together with the materials necessary for the carrying out of its functions.[388]

The members of each *section syndicale* may meet once a month within the business but not in the working areas;[389] the representatives may meet during the hours that they are allocated for their roles as delegates, but otherwise union meetings occur outside working hours.[390]

Currently a majority vote (*accord majoritaire*) is required mainly for decisions relating to the working hours. For other matters, the signature of minority unions representing 30% of the employees is sufficient, provided that the unions representing the majorities do not object.

From 1 May 2018 it is intended that the *accord majoritaire* will be the standard for all matters.

An employer may organise a referendum to validate an *accord* that has been signed by the unions representing more than 30% of the employees in the enterprise, unless all of the signatory unions oppose the referendum. Previously such a referendum could only be started by the employees' representatives.

---

383 art. L.2141-1 C. trav. et art. L.2141-5 C. trav.
384 art. L.2141-3 C. trav.
385 art. L.2121-1 C. trav.
386 art. L.2122-1 C. trav.
387 art. L.2142-1 C. trav.
388 art. L.2142-8 C. trav.
389 art. L.2142-10 C. trav.
390 art. L.2142-11 C. trav.

1) Union delegate – *Délégué syndical*

In businesses or establishments that have had at least 50 employees for 12 months, consecutive or otherwise, in the previous 3 years, and have a *section syndicale*, a representative union may appoint 1 or more delegates (the numbers allowed usually depend upon the number of employees, and are up to set limits) selected from employees who received at least 10% of the votes in the first round of the elections for the *CSE*. In some circumstances if there is no person who is eligible on that basis, the union may pick a delegate from the other candidates or if none, from its members there. Businesses with several establishments of at least 50 employees may have in addition a central delegate.[391]

The delegates shall be given the time necessary to carry out their role (which is paid by the employer),[392] which will be no less than:

50 to 150 employees – 12 hours per month
151–499 employees – 18 hours per month
500 or more employees – 24 hours per month.[393]

There is also an additional amount of hours for each *section syndicale*, where the delegates are called to negotiate a *convention* or *accord d'entreprise*.[394]

For businesses with fewer than 50 employees, the representative unions in that business may appoint a member of the delegation of the *CSE* to also be the union delegate for the time that the person holds their mandate as *CSE* delegate. Such a delegate shall not receive an additional allotment of hours for the additional role.[395]

2) Representative of the union section – *Répresentant de la section syndicale*

A *répresentant de la section syndicale* may be selected by a union to be the representative of the union section in a business/establishment of at least 50 employees, where the union is not yet sufficiently representative to be eligible for certain matters. The representative will have broadly the same roles and benefits as a delegate, but may not negotiate *accords collectifs*. The idea is that this may enable the union to seek to obtain enough support to become "representative". If however the union continues not to have sufficient support following the next elections, the employee loses their mandate as *répresentant*.[396]

---

391 art. L.2143-3 C. trav.
392 art. L.2143-17 C. trav.
393 art. L.2143-13 C. trav.
394 art. L.2143-16 C. trav.
395 art. L.2143-6 C. trav.
396 art. L.2142-1-1 C. trav.

C) Internal representatives and representative bodies

Recent reforms intend to fuse a number of these roles into 1 body, the social and economic committee (*comité social et économique*). It will consolidate and continue all the roles of the 3 previous types of representatives and have their powers and can be the subject of legal proceedings.

Until recently the previous bodies have included the delegates of the employees (*délégués du personnel – DP*), the enterprise committee (*comité d'entreprise – CE*) and the committee for hygiene, safety and working conditions (*comité d'hygiène, de sécurité et des conditions de travail – CHSCT*).

A period of gradual evolution will be allowed.

For reference only, the old rules relating to the old representative bodies are set out in an appendix.

Social and economic committee – *Comité social et économique* (*CSE*)

The new *CSE* will be set up in any enterprise with at least 11 employees and becomes obligatory once there have been 11 employees for 12 consecutive months.[397] Its roles and powers are broadly related to the number of employees, whether more or fewer than 50.

In enterprises with at least 11 and fewer than 50 employees, the roles will be as follows:[398]

- presenting individual or collective claims regarding salary, the application of the *Code du travail* and other legal dispositions notably concerning social protection, as well as any *conventions* or *accords* applicable in the enterprise

- contributing to promoting health and safety at work and working conditions in the enterprise, and carry out enquiries into work accidents or work-related illness

- in a *société anonyme* when the members of the delegation of the personnel of the *CSE* present claims which cannot be dealt with after deliberation by the *conseil d'administration*, they will upon their request meet with them in the presence of the manager(s) or their representative

- taking all complaints/claims and observations to the work inspectors that relate to legal rules for which the *CSE* is responsible for assuring control.

All workers (including part time and e.g. those on work placements) retain

---

397 art. L.2311-2 C. trav.
398 art. L.2312-5 C. trav.

the right to present their own issues to the employer or the employer's representatives.[399]

The mission[400] of the *CSE* is to ensure a collective voice for the employees to have their interests taken into account in decisions relating to the management and the financial and economic development of the enterprise, as well as the organisation of the work, professional training and production techniques.

The committee is to be informed and consulted on questions relating to the organisation and general running of the enterprise, and particularly about:

1) measures that by their nature affect the number or the organisation of the workers
2) modification of its economic or legal organisation
3) conditions of work including working hours and training
4) introduction of new technologies, all important changes modifying health and safety and work and working conditions
5) measures taken with a view to facilitating work, e.g. after an accident at work, for those injured in war, for people with progressive chronic illnesses.

The committee should be consulted[401] on various matters including:

1) strategic orientations for the enterprise
2) the economic and financial situation of the enterprise
3) the social set-up of the enterprise and conditions of work and employment
4) restructuring and reduction of the workforce
5) group dismissals for economic reasons
6) an offer of public acquisition
7) procedures to safeguard the enterprise, liquidation etc.

The committee has a right to issue an alert in various situations such as if there is a risk to personal rights, physical or mental health or individual freedoms; grave or imminent danger regarding public health and the environment; or if it has knowledge of facts that are of a nature that would noticeably affect the economic situation of the enterprise, or of facts that might indicate an abusive recourse to *CDD*s.

There are also various other consultative and representative roles. 2 members of the *CSE* also attend in a consultative capacity at all meetings of the *conseil d'administration* or the *conseil de surveillance*, as well as general assemblies.

---

399 art. L.2312-7 C. trav.
400 art. L.2312-8 C. trav.
401 art. L.2312-17 C. trav.

Members of the *CSE*

The *CSE* is made up of the employer and a delegation of the personnel, involving a number of the members set by *décret* taking into account the number of employees.

The delegation is made up of an equal number of position holders (*titulaires*) and deputies (*suppléants*). The deputies attend meetings when the position holder is absent.[402] In enterprises with fewer than 300 employees the union delegate will also be a member. Where there are more than 300 employees in an enterprise, each union that is representative in the enterprise or the establishment may designate a member.[403]

The work doctor and the relevant member of the safety service attend the *CSE* meetings that relate to health, safety and work conditions.

Once the number of employees reaches more than 11, every 4 years elections will be held for the members.[404] Below that number of employees, elections are not mandatory. The *CSE* can also be put together by a *convention* or an *accord collectif.*

Finance

The *CSE* has 2 budgets funded by the employer, one for running/organising itself and another budget for social and cultural activities.

In businesses of 50–1,999 employees, the first of the above budget is set at 0.2% of the gross salaries, and in businesses larger than that at 0.22%. The social and cultural budget is usually set by an *accord d'entreprise.*

Delegation hours

The employees on the *CSE* have a credit of hours (that are paid as ordinary work hours) to carry out their delegated functions.[405]

There are set usual minima:

In enterprises with fewer than 50 employees – 10 hours per month
50 or more employees – 16 hours per month.

Training

Employees elected to the *CSE* for the first time are entitled to a maximum of 5 days' training for this role. This time is paid as normal working time.

Protection

Members may not be penalised or dismissed for reasons relating to their membership or duties of the *CSE*.

---

402 art. L.2314-1 C. trav.
403 art. L.2314-2 C. trav.
404 art. L.2341-4 C. trav.
405 art. L.2315 C. trav.

D) Work health service – *Service de santé au travail* (*SST*)

Employers must set up[406] and pay for[407] a work health service, whose purpose is to take steps to preserve the health of employees and to advise employees how to ensure that their work does not adversely affect their health, including where relevant ensuring oversight by the relevant authorities.[408]

E) Participatory interprofessional regional commissions – *Commissions paritaires régionales interprofessionnelle*[409]

This is a new type of body which applies to businesses with fewer than 11 employees from branches that do not have regional or, where relevant, departmental participatory commissions.

Their purpose is to give to employees and employers all information and/or advice that may be useful to them regarding legal and *conventionnelles* rules that may apply to them, to give advice on questions specific to businesses with fewer than 10 employees, and their employees, and to make suggestions regarding social and cultural activities.

They will be composed of 20 members: 10 from employees' unions, 10 from employers' organisations.

The commission members are appointed for 4 years, which is renewable.

F) Work social service – *Service social du travail*

In businesses where there are usually at least 250 employees, a *service social de travail* must be set up.[410] Its purpose is to ensure and facilitate the private life of the employees. It collaborates with the *SST* and liaises with the welfare bodies and those that assist and deal with the finding of positions, with a view to assisting employees in exercising the rights that legislation gives them.[411]

---

406 art. L.4622-1 C. trav.
407 art. L.4622-6 C. trav.
408 art. L.4622-2 C. trav.
409 loi Rebsamen, ou loi n° 2015-994 du 17 août 2015
410 art. L.4631-1 C. trav.
411 art. L.4631-2 C. trav.

G) Protection of the representatives of the employees against dismissal

The representatives generally have additional protection against being dismissed.[412] In many cases the authorisation of the *inspecteur du travail* must be obtained prior to any such dismissal. The usual procedures for dismissal will also apply.

---

412 art. L.2411-1 et seq. C. trav.

24. Collective disputes – *Conflits collectifs*

A) The strike – *La grève*

La grève in legal terms, to fulfil the requirements for legal protection of the employees, occurs where work stops completely, collectively and deliberately to defend work-based claims (e.g. remuneration, work conditions).[413]

A go-slow may be described as a *grève perlée* and will not usually fulfil the definition of a strike,[414] nor would a situation where work is carried out in a voluntarily defective manner be a strike as the work continues to occur.[415] A *grève tournante* occurs where stops affect successive parts of the service of the enterprise; this may be legal in some cases, however it would be deemed an abuse (as would a series of short strikes carried out at a variable rhythm) if the intention is to damage the enterprise.

At least 2 employees must be involved for the action to be classified as being a strike. 1 person taking action will only constitute a strike if they are striking as part of a national movement.[416] The strike may involve only a minority of the workforce[417] or 1 section of it (e.g. 1 category of personnel).

Strikes which are for political aims and not for work-based matters would not fulfil the definition.

A *grève de solidarité* is where the employees are not striking for their own employment aims, but in support of another employee. It is not a strike if the claims do not relate to the striking employees themselves but purely to seek the re-employment of another employee who has been lawfully dismissed.[418]

---

413 Cass. soc. 18 juin 1996
414 Soc. 18 févr. 1960, n°57-40.746 P : JCP 1060. II. 11704, note F.D. ; Dr. Soc. 1960.490. obs. H.F.
415 Soc. 22 avr. 1964, n°61-40.673 P : JCP 1964. II. 13883 note B. A.
416 Soc. 29 mars 1995 n° 93-41.863. P RJS 1995.369 n° 553
417 Soc. 3 oct. 1963: GADT, 4ed, n° 188; D. 1964. 3, note G. Lyon-Caen
418 Soc. 8 janv. 1965, n°64-40.135 P : Dr. Soc. 1965n 380, obs. J. Savatier

B) Protection of the right to strike

The right to strike is a constitutional right (*droit constitutionnel*) arising initially from the 1946 Constitution (*Constitution*) and then confirmed in the 1958 Constitution. It is not set out in that way in the *Code du travail,* although the legal protection for the proper organising and carrying out of a strike is.

The legal use of strikes is different in the private and the public sectors;[419] some types of employee are excluded from the right to strike, e.g. police personnel,[420] personnel in the external services of the prison services, the military,[421] judicial magistrates.[422]

With certain limited exceptions for certain types of work, a private sector strike may be started by employees at any moment once the work-related demands have been brought to the attention of the employer. The employees do not have to wait for a response from the employer.

In the public sector, 5 days' notice must be given by those intending to strike, setting out the reasons for the strike and the proposed geographical areas, time and length. During this notice period the parties are obliged to negotiate.[423] A minimum service must also be assured in certain sectors, e.g. public transport.

Any disciplinary action because of the strike (and in the absence of *faute lourde* by the employee) will be null.[424] *Faute lourde* would include acts of violence, locking in managers, damaging goods or intrusions on the freedom to work.

Time spent on strike is usually unpaid.[425] *Jours fériés* and *chômés* do not have to be paid if they fall within the strike period. Pay reduction must be exactly calculated to reflect only the strike period. The employer and employee may however agree to payment or part payment during strike periods.

The employer may not cover the striking workers by replacing them with employees on *CDD*s or temporary workers (*travailleurs intérimaires*).[426]

Where the employer closes the enterprise temporarily (a lock-out – *le lock-out*) in response to an imminent or actual collective conflict it may only be legal if the employer can show the impossibility of running the enterprise because of the strike or for safety reasons, otherwise it may be found to be in effect a type of sanction in that for example it prevents the employees working; hence it will be deemed to be illegal.

---

419 for the public sector, see art. L.2512-1 C. trav. and the following articles
420 loi 48-1505 29 septembre 1948
421 art. L.4121-4 C. défense
422 art. 10 loi 58-1270 du 22 décembre 1958
423 art. L.2512-2 C. trav.
424 art. L.1132-2 et art. L.2511-1 C. trav.
425 Soc. 21 déc. 1977: Bull. civ. V. n°726; D. 1978. IR 75
426 art. L.1242-6 C. trav.

25. Breaking the contract – *La rupture du contrat de travail*

A fixed term contract (*contrat à durée déterminé*) will end at the conclusion of its term/minimum term/purpose, as applicable.[427]

To end a contract before its conclusion is known as anticipated rupture (*rupture anticipé*). For a *CDD* this will usually only be allowed in cases of *faute grave*, *force majeure* or medical incapacity to carry out the work (there is for example a limited procedure for engineers and *cadres* who have been recruited in certain circumstances to complete particular types of task).[428]

The employee may terminate the contract by handing in their notice (*démission*) or by a form of constructive dismissal due to the fault of the employer, which is described as a unilateral break – *une rupture unilatérale*.

If the employee terminates the contract by reason of a failure of obligation(s) on the part of the employer, this is viewed as a different process known as *une prise d'acte* (taking action). This can be construed either as a dismissal (*licenciement*) if there is real and serious cause and the facts support this, or otherwise as a *démission*[429] – which is essentially a resignation in this case similar to constructive dismissal. Following such action, the employee may then need to apply to a judge to rule on the situation.

Any court application regarding the termination of a contract must usually be brought within 12 months of the notification of the termination.[430]

The termination may also be by mutual consent, for example the *rupture conventionnelle* or *la transaction* (mutual arrangement dealing with the consequences of a dismissal previously notified, handing in of notice or a court process).

There are only 2 recognised ways of justifying a dismissal: *licenciement pour motif personnel* (a reason relating to the individual concerned) and *licenciement économique* (economic reasons).

It is also possible for the employee to seek a judicial termination (*rupture judiciaire*); the employer may also do this.[431]

---

427 art. L.1243-5 C. trav.
428 art. L.1243-1 C. trav.
429 Cass. soc. 25 juin 2003, Dr. Soc, p.823
430 art. L.1471-1 C. trav.
431 E.g. usually required in application of art. L.6222-18 C. trav.

A) Notice periods – *Délai de préavis*

The employee should respect any notice period (*préavis*) set out as relevant to that type of contract by the Code, by any law, by any applicable collective agreement or, if none of the above, by custom.[432]

The employer will tend to have to respect certain basic minimum notice periods to the employee, which usually vary depending upon the length of employment of the employee. Where the dismissal is not for *faute grave* the notice period minimums set by the Code are usually:[433]

- less than 6 months' work: as set by law, *convention*; *accord* or in default by custom in the locality and in the profession

and then only if the law, *convention, accord collectif,* contract or custom do not provide a notice period or a length of service provision that is more favourable to the employee:

- 6 months to 2 years: 1 month
- at least 2 years: 2 months.

A *CDD* may usually only be terminated in advance of its usual term by either party in cases of mutual agreement, *faute grave, force majeure*, or medical incapacity.[434]

Some contracts such as *VRPs* have different minimum set notice periods by either party, which may depend upon the length of employment.[435]

Employees carrying out *travail temporaire* will also have to comply with set notice period minima.[436]

The notice period is suspended if the employee is unable to work by virtue of an accident at work.[437]

An employee who fails to respect the notice period may be ordered to pay compensation equal to the amount of the remuneration they would have received during the period not worked.

In some circumstances the law allows the employee to dispense with the notice period, for example with pregnant women.[438]

The employer may usually allow the employee not to comply with the obligation provided the employee suffers no financial loss as a result.

---

432 art. L.1237-1 C. trav.
433 art. L.1234-1 C. trav.
434 art. L.1243-1 C. trav.
435 art. L.7313-9 C. trav.
436 art. L.1251-28 C. trav.
437 Soc. 18 juill. 1996, n°93-43.581 P : JCP 1996 II. 22726, note Corrignan-Carsin
438 art. L.1225-34 C. trav.

B) Giving notice by an employee – *La démission*

Démission is the unilateral termination of the work contract by the employee. The intention of the employee should be clear and unequivocal but it need not be substantiated by a reason. It must be genuine, and freely given, otherwise it may be deemed to be null.[439] When the termination is deemed to be null, the contract is deemed never to have been broken. Unexplained absence by the employee, of whatever length, does not show the intention required and will not constitute *démission*.

A termination of the contract by the employee because of the non-respect by the employer of one of the essential elements of the contract will be deemed to be terminated due to the employer.

There are various procedures for a *démission* set out in the *Code du travail* which vary depending upon the type of contract, and in many cases rules may become applicable by virtue for example of any law, a collective agreement, the work contract or custom.

There is not always a requirement for a notice given by an employee to be in writing. Thus it can be verbal. In practice, however, notification will usually be expected to be in writing because of terms found in *conventions collectives*.

C) Incorrect termination of the contract by the employee – *Démission abusive*

If the employee incorrectly terminates the contract and causes loss or damage to the employer as a result, they may be ordered to pay damages and interest by the *tribunaux*.[440]

If in circumstances of an abusive termination by the employee, the employee is taken on by a new employer, the new employer may become jointly liable for the compensation if:

- the new employer participated in the termination
- the new employer employed the employee knowing that the employee was still bound by the preceding contract
- the new employer continues to use the employee after finding out that the employee is still bound by the preceding contract (but not if, by the time the employer knew, the previous contract had finished).[441]

---

439 Cass. soc. 29 janvier 2003, *RJS*, 04/2003, n° 424; also art. L.1152-3 C. trav. which specifically sets out that all termination of the contract that results from *harcèlement moral* (bullying) is null
440 art. L.1237-2 C. trav.
441 art. L.1237-3 C. trav.

26. Termination of the contract because of fault of the employer – *La rupture du contrat de travail pour faute de l'employeur*

A) Basis

The contract of employment involves reciprocal obligations. Articles 1224–1230 of the *Code civil* apply. Thus, a party to whom an obligation is not fulfilled may as a general rule:

- oblige the other party to carry out their obligation
- seek a court order for damages and interest.

In employment situations there may not always be an obligation to continue the work contract.

A settlement should be attempted before taking legal proceedings; refusal to do so may count against a party who has refused.

B) Employer's faults – *Fautes de l'employeur*

Broadly speaking, the employer has 3 primary obligations, being to:
1) pay the remuneration due, when it is due
2) provide the work contracted for
3) act with good faith.

A serious failure to carry out any of the above obligations may constitute a breach of the contract due to the fault of the employer (*une rupture du contrat de travail aux torts de l'employeur*). Examples would include physical or psychological violence by the employer or failure by the employer to comply with safety obligations towards the employee. Broadly, for the breach to entitle the employee to ask the court to consider it effectively a dismissal, the breach would need to be of a nature that prevents the continuance of the work contract.

C) Consequences

If the employer is held to be at fault, the breach leads to the consequences of a *licenciement sans cause réelle et sérieuse* (dismissal for no real or serious cause).

If the employer is held not to be at fault, then the termination may be deemed to be a *rupture abusive* – abusive termination – by the employee. Either result may lead to damages for the injured party.

27. Negotiated departure (*le départ négocié*) and *transaction*

A) Negotiated departure

The parties may agree between themselves to an uncontested termination of the contract. If the reason is for economic reasons related to the work, then the employer should usually comply with the rules relating to dismissal for this reason.

B) *La transaction*

The *transaction* is an agreement, in this case a settlement of court proceedings occurring between the employer and employee. It would set out the consequences of the termination of the contract. It should be completed after the termination and set out the mutual concessions. It ends the proceedings.

The agreement gives authority to the arrangement.

C) Termination of the contract by convention – *La rupture conventionnelle*

This is an agreement by which the employer and the employee (usually only those in the private sector may do this) decide to terminate the employment without court proceedings.[442] It is not deemed to be either a dismissal or a *démission*. It may be used both for individual and for collective terminations.[443]

This type of agreement may not apply to certain *ruptures économiques* where there is an *accord collectif de gestion prévisionnelle des emplois et des compétences* (provisional collective *accord* for the management of employment and competences), or to breaks that arise from *un plan de sauvegarde de emploi*.[444]

---

442 art. L.1237-11 C. trav.
443 art. L.1237-17 C. trav.
444 art. L.1237-16 C. trav.

The process is set out in the *Loi du 25 juin 2008* and the Code. Initially there must be a meeting or meetings[445] at which the employee may be accompanied, and if so the employer may also, and which leads to the signature of a *convention*. The *convention* sets out the conditions to be applied, including the amount of the *indemnité*.[446] The *indemnité conventionnelle* paid to the employee must not be less than the *indemnité légale de licenciement*.[447]

The parties each have a period of 15 days from the signature within which they may withdraw.[448] At the end of this period the *convention* must be sent to the *direction départmentale du travail et de l'emploi (DDTE)*[449] to be formalised (*homologué*). If there is no response from the *DDTE* in 15 days from receipt by the *DDTE* then formalisation is deemed to have occurred.

The contents may be contested before a judge in the year following the formalisation.[450]

---

445 art. L.1237-12 C. trav.
446 art. L.1237-13 C. trav.
447 art. L.1237-13 and L.1234-9 C. trav.
448 art. L.1237-13 C. trav.
449 art. L.1237-14 C. trav.
450 art. L.1237-14 C.trav.

28. Appendix

N.B. This section relates to the representatives that existed prior to recent legal reforms. There is a temporary period during which they may continue to exist in certain circumstances. This appendix is for general information only.

1) Employees' delegates – *Délégués du personnel (DP)*

Where an enterprise has at least 11 employees at the same time in 12 months, consecutive or not, in the last 3 years, it is mandatory to have *DP*s, elected for 4 years. Businesses with fewer than 11 employees may nevertheless choose by *accord* or *convention* to have *DP*s and there are circumstances when the administrative authority may impose the election of *DP*s. In enterprises with fewer than 50 employees, the "representative unions" applicable may appoint a *DP*, for the period of their mandate as *DP*, as union delegates.

The election process involves 2 stages of voting: in the first stage, the unions may present a list of candidates. If the number of voters is insufficient, a second round of voting is held for which any employee may present themselves as a candidate.

The *DP* is otherwise separate from the union delegate (*délégué syndical*), whose role is to run all union matters, to represent the union members to the employer and to participate in the collective negotiation.

The number of *DP*s depends amongst other things upon the total number of employees in the enterprise or in that particular establishment. For each *délégué titulaire* (delegate holding the post) there must also be a deputy (*délégué suppléant*), who will only take active part if the *délégué titulaire* cannot act.

The *DP*s may be elected in respect of each distinct establishment or per economic and social unit.

Where establishments have fewer than 11 employees but on the same site at least 50 employees work continuously (e.g. an industrial zone, a shopping centre, a worksite), if there are problems common to the businesses on the site the *directeur départemental du travail* may impose the election of *DP*s.

Role of the delegate

The *DP* presents the individual and collective representations and claims of the employees with regard to salaries, the application of the *Code du travail* and other rules and legislation, and with regard to remuneration, hygiene and safety and *conventions* and *accords collectifs*.

The *DP* may and should take all complaints to the works inspector and all other matters that fall within the inspector's competence.

The *DP* represents claims of permanent employees in the establishment, and also employees of external enterprises and temporary employees with regard to conditions of work in the establishment.

The *DP* works with the *comité d'entreprise* (works council) and the *comité d'hygiène de sécurité et des conditions de travail* where they exist.

Employees should consult the *DP* about matters such as the *plan de formation*, dismissals for economic reasons, *reclassement* of an employee after an accident at work, holiday dates etc.

Additional roles

In various circumstances when there is no *comité d'entreprise* the *DP*s carry out all or part of its economic functions.

The *Code du travail* sets out various situations where the *DP*s should be consulted regarding various different matters (e.g. dismissal of part of the workforce, plans for dismissal for economic reasons, derogation from maximum working time etc.).

Differences apply between businesses where there are fewer than 50 employees and ones that have 50 or more.

Where there is no *CHST*, the *DP*s may also become responsible for all or part of its roles, and have the same means, methods and obligations as that body would have.

Powers and procedures

Once a month (or at the request of the *DPs)* the employer must have a meeting to which all the *DP*s, including the deputies (the *DPs*) should be invited.

The *DP*s should notify the employer in writing of all requests 2 working days before the meeting. The employer should respond in writing giving reasons, within six *jours ouvrables*.

Where there is risk or damage to the personal rights of people, to their physical or mental health, of individual freedoms in the enterprise which is not justified by the nature of the task to be accomplished or proportionate to the purpose to be accomplished, the *DPs* should immediately alert the employer.

Time spent in the meetings counts as work time and is paid as such. The employer must allow the *DPs* the time needed to carry out their functions up to certain usual limits, which depend generally upon the number of employees:

fewer than 50 employees – 10 hours per month
at least 50 employees – 15 hours

where there is no *CE* and the *DP* is carrying out what would be the *CE*'s economic roles – 20 hours per month.

These hours are to be used for the benefit of the role and there is a presumption that they are so used.

The *DP* should be provided with an area for their role and for having meetings and notice boards where they can put up information for the employees.

DPs are entitled to freedom to go about either inside or outside the workplace for the purpose of the fulfilment of their duties. They are entitled to put up notices setting out matters that it is their responsibility to draw to the attention of the workforce, in the workplace and at the entries to the workplaces.

An employer who interferes or tries to interfere with the free choice by employees of the *DPs* or the regular exercise of their duties faces a potential fine of 7,500 euros and, with regard to the choice of *DPs*, also a possible prison sentence of 1 year.

2) Works council – *Comité d'entreprise (CE)*

Where an enterprise has had at least 50 employees in 12 months, whether consecutive or not, in the 3 preceding years, there must be a *CE*. Where there are fewer than 50 employees, a *CE* may be created by *accord collectif*. Where the enterprise has several separate establishments, each one should have its own *comité d'établissement* in addition to which there should be 1 acting across the enterprise (*comité centrale d'entreprise*).

The *CE* has a civil personality and manages its own budget. The employer provides a fund (known as a *subvention de fonctionnement*) equal to 0.2% of the total salaries, and a contribution to pay for social and cultural events.

Members are entitled to be paid their usual remuneration for the time spent by the members dealing with the meetings. The employer must provide a place and the equipment necessary for the *CE* to use to carry out its functions.

Composition

The *chef d'entreprise* or their representative will be party to the *CE*. They will be the president of the committee and may have 2 deputies who will have a consultative role only. There will also be elected employees' representatives (plus en equal number of deputies), who are elected for 4 years (both the holders of the post and the deputies, whose role at meetings is consultative). The number of these will depend upon the numbers in the business. There will be union representatives from each union at the business, who will be entitled to attend meetings but only to be consulted. The committee will elect a secretary and a treasurer in conditions set out in a *décret*.

The election process involves 2 stages of voting: in the first stage, the unions may present a list of candidates. If the number of voters is insufficient, a second round of voting is held for which any employee may present themselves as a candidate.

The number of elected representatives depends upon the number in the workforce and will be set out by *décret*, but there should be at least 3 holders and 3 deputies.

Role

The main role is to ensure that the collective wishes of the employees are represented so that the employer can take their interests into account when making decisions relative to the management and to economic and financial evolution of the business, the organisation of work, work training and the techniques of production. It has no decision-making powers itself.

The *CE* should be consulted when questions arise regarding the general running of the business and before a decision is taken. This may for example include economic or legal changes, steps that might affect the size or structure of the workforce, paid holiday, and length and organisation of work time.

The *CE* may also under its own initiative or at the request of the employer, put forward proposals for the improvement of the conditions of for example work, employment and training.

The *CE* will also be involved in carrying out reviews of and organising social and cultural activities including for example the work restaurant. It may also choose to participate in funding them.

Procedures and powers

Where the enterprise has at least 300 employees the employer must call a meeting of the *CE* every month. Where there are fewer than 300, the meetings should be at least once every 2 months. A majority of the members may call a second meeting. Where the employer fails to call meetings, the *inspecteur du travail* may call a meeting with the employer and sit in on the meeting if at least half the members request this.

The employer must consult the *CE* annually regarding the activity of the business, the development of the employment, the conditions of the employment of the men and the women and steps taken on behalf of disabled employees, training, holidays, salaries and so on. The committee is entitled to have the assistance of an accountant. The *CE* is entitled to submit responses and alternative suggestions.

All members of the *CE* are entitled to be heard at the meeting but only the elected members and the employer have the right to vote.

The members of the *CE* are bound by rules of confidentiality and the duty to protect trade secrets.

The *CE* may set up separate commissions if it chooses, to deal with particular issues. It may also consult experts. In addition the *CE* may organise meetings within the enterprise, dealing with current issues, and there are provisions enabling external people to be invited under certain conditions.

The *CE* has a right to request the employer to provide explanations and to make notifications if it becomes aware of facts that may affect the economic situation of the enterprise.

To exercise their functions, the members of the *CE*, and in businesses of at least 500 employees the union representatives, and the union representatives to the *comité central d'entreprise* for groups of businesses which jointly have 500 employees but where each individually does not, have a credit of 20 working hours per month for time for the *CE*.

3) Consolidated representative body – *La délégation unique du personnel (DUP)*

In enterprises with fewer than 300 employees, the employer (after consultation with the *délégués du personnel*, and, if it exists, the *CE* and the *CHSCT*) may fuse the *CE*, the *CHSCT* and the *DP* into 1 delegation – the *DUP*. Since the *CE* and *CHSCT* will usually only exist in businesses with 50 or more employees, the *DUP* will not usually be relevant to businesses of fewer than 50.

The *DUP* is elected using broadly the same procedures as for the *CE* and the procedural rules are broadly the same for each of the previous functions. The members retain their roles and powers in the same form within the *DUP*. The *DUP* should meet every 2 months, and at least 4 of these meetings should deal with matters relevant to the *CHSCT*. Each member is entitled to a work time credit that will take into account the roles of each body and for which usual maxima will be set by *décret*.

4) The committee for hygiene, security and work conditions – *Le comité d'hygiène de sécurité et des conditions de travail (CHSCT)*

This is obligatory in all enterprises or establishments with at least 50 employees. In the absence of such a body, the *DE* takes on the role and powers.

The *CHSCT* is composed of the *chef d'entreprise* as president and a delegation of employees selected from the *DP*(s) and the members of the *CE*, elected by them. The number of delegates depends upon the size of the workforce.

The purpose of the *CHSCT* is to supervise the protection of the health of the employees, their safety and the improvement of working conditions and to monitor compliance with legal requirements in these regards.

To carry out their mission the delegates have a credit of hours which varies according to the size of the workforce, the minimum for establishments of up to 99 employees being 2 hours per month and increasing thereafter. The allowable hours spent on these duties are paid at the same rate as the normal remuneration.

No budget as such is provided for, but the employer must provide what is necessary including the means, for the preparation and organisation of the relevant procedures and meetings (including a suitable meeting area) and for any external visits, to enable the committee to do what is required by inquiries or inspections.

The *CHSCT* has a *pouvoir d'alerte*. This is a process with several stages. First, a member of the committee, either directly or by receiving information from an employee, becomes aware of a grave and imminent cause of danger. The member then immediately notifies the employer or the employer's representative. The employer then puts in process an inquiry with that member and informs the representative of what follows.

References

Code du travail, Legifrance and Editions Tissot

travail-emploi.gouv.fr
www.entreprises.cci-paris-idf.fr/web/reglementation/developpement-
    entreprise/droit-social/les-indemnites-de-conges-payes
www.larousse.com/en/dictionnaires/francais-anglais/RTT/723277

Termes juridiques Dalloz
European Commission www.ec.europa.eu

Thanks to David Hardie (DRTC, ARCST, MInstMC, FIChemE, CEng) for editorial assistance; Benjamin Kidd (BSc, MSc) and Sean Waters (LLB) (Solicitor) for software and extensive practical assistance; Karen Allen for proof-reading assistance.

Terminology, French–English/ English–French

French	English
accord	agreement of wishes with a view to achieve a legal effect sought by the parties to the agreement
accord collectif de gestion prévisionnelle des emplois et des compétences	provisional collective accord for the management of employment and competences
accord d'entreprise	agreement between the employer and the representatives of the employees/union there
accord de branche	agreement between one or more of the employers and one or more of the representatives of the employees (usually unions) in a given sector of work
acte	document or action leading to a legal effect
adaptation des salaries à leur poste de travail	suitability of employees to job
affection	use for a particular purpose
AFPA (l'Association nationale pour la formation professionnelle des adultes)	National association for adult training
agent de maitrise	a work category set out in *conventions collectives*. Their role will be to direct, coordinate, or control the work of a certain number of *ouvriers*. There is not a precise legal definition
agissements répétés	repeated behaviour
allocation chômage	unemployment benefit

amplitude journalière	total length of the effective working time (as defined) from start to end of the working day, plus breaks, meal times, interruptions
ANAEM (l'Agence national de l'accueil des étrangers et des migrants)	national agency for assisting foreigners and migrants
ancienneté	length of employment
ANPE (l'Agence nationale pour l'emploi)	former body now merged with the *ASSEDIC* into the *Pôle emploi*
APE (Activité Principale Exercée)	principal activity from a set list of codes
apprentissage	apprenticeships (specific types of work placements specifically to lead to particular types of qualification i.e. in particular professional or technological diplomas of the second level or superior or a type of professional qualification)
ASSEDIC (Association pour l'emploi dans l'industrie et le commerce)	former body Association for Employment in Industry and Trade now merged with the *ANPE* into the *Pôle emploi*
assignation	writ, summons
assurance chômage	unemployment benefit – can also refer to unemployment insurance
avertissment	warning
avocat	French lawyer, professional qualification similar to solicitor, including advocacy but not covering all the same aspects of the legal profession
blâme	reprimand, usually in the form of a written warning and tending to be serious including a final warning
bulletin de salaire	wage slip
cadre	a term denoting either an employee receiving over a certain minimum salary, or having a certain level of professional qualification
caisse de mutualité agricole	agricultural mutual

caisse de retraite complémentaire	pension scheme supplementary to the state one
carte de résident	residence permit (10-year duration)
carte de séjour temporaire	short-term residence permit
cause réelle et sérieuse	real and serious cause
CDD (contrat de travail à durée déterminée)	fixed term contract
centre de formation des apprentis/CFA	apprentice training centre
certificat d'investissement	a type of share
chambre civile	civil court section
chambre commerciale	commercial court section
chambre correctionnelle	criminal court section
chambre d'accusation	section of the *Cour d'appel* dealing with appeals related to the jurisdictional aspects of criminal matters
chambre sociale	dealing with so-called social matters *(droit social)*
charge	criminal charge/accusation
charge de la preuve	burden of proof
classement	the classification of the employee in a deemed level or category of work
clause d'objectifs	object clause
clause de garantie d'emploi	guarantee of employment clause
code APE (Activité Principale Exercée)	code for the principal activity from a set list of codes
Code civil	Civil Code
Code de commerce	Code of Commerce
Code de travail	Code of Employment Law
Code pénal	Penal Code

collectivités territoriales	public bodies that are separate from the State and have legal autonomy and own and manage their own resources
collégiale (f)	comprising more than one judge/magistrate etc.
comité centrale d'entreprise	the central *comité d'entreprise* for the group, where a business comprises several establishments
comité d'entreprise (CE)	works council
comité d'établissement	the *comité d'entreprise* for each establishment in a business comprising several establishments
comité d'hygiène, de sécurité et des conditions de travail (CHSCT)	committee for health and safety and work conditions
comité social et économique (CSE)	social and economic committee
commission paritaire régionale interprofessionnelle	regional joint inter-professional commission – composed of representatives from both employees' unions and employers' groups, to advise and assist employees of and employers of businesses with fewer than 11 employees
commune	lowest local administrative division in France
compte d'engagement citoyen	record of charitable/voluntary work
compte épargne-temps (CET)	holiday account
concurrence	competition
conflit collectif	collective conflict
congé	holiday/leave
congé d'adoption	adoption leave
congé de mobilité	mobility time off, to help employees return to stable work by seeking assistance, training and work. Applies to businesses with at least 100 employees and who have reached an

	accord collectif about plans to manage the jobs and the skills
congé de reclassement	time off for training, to take steps to seek other work etc.; applicable in businesses of at least 1,000 employees
congé de solidarité familiale	leave for a death
congé individuel de formation (CIF)	personal leave for training
congé lié à la naissance ou à l'adoption d'un enfant	leave related to the birth or adoption of a child
congé lié à la naissance ou à l'adoption d'un enfant	leave related to the marriage of a child
congé lié au décès du père, de la mere, d'un frère, d'une soeur, du beau-père, de la belle-mère du salarié	holiday related to the death of a father, mother, brother, sister, father-in-law or mother-in-law of the employee
congé lié au mariage du salarié	leave related to the marriage of the employee
congé de maternité	maternity leave
congé d'education parentale	parental education leave
congé de paternité	paternity leave
congé payé	paid holiday
congé postnatal	maternity leave after the birth
congé pour création d'entreprise	leave to set up a business
congé pour un enfant malade	holiday for a sick child
congé prénatal	maternity leave prior to the birth
congé principal	main holiday
congé sabbatique	sabbatical
Conseil d'État	"The Conseil d'État advises the Government on the preparation of bills, ordinances and certain decrees. It also answers the

Government's queries on legal affairs and conducts studies upon the request of the Government or through its own initiative regarding administrative or public policy issues.

"Conseil d'État is the highest administrative jurisdiction – it is the final arbiter of cases relating to executive power, local authorities, independent public authorities, public administration agencies or any other agency invested with public authority." http://www.conseil-etat.fr/en/

conseil de discipline	disciplinary panel
Constitution	Constitution
contingent annuel d'heures supplémentaires	total supplementary hours over a year
contrat	contract
contrat d'accompagnement dans l'emploi (CAE) (also CIE)	contract where a subsidy is provided to the employer for the job, generally to enable those who are having difficulties finding employment for either social reasons or reasons relating to the area of work – usually retail sector
contrat d'apprentissage	apprenticeship contract
contrat d'avenir (CA)	type of contract particularly aimed at helping young people having various types of difficulty obtaining work, involving subsidy to the employer and additional support for the employee by e.g. tutors in the business and assistance from State bodies
contrat de chantier ou d'opération	contract for a project or job of work – previously mainly for construction industry but now for general use as well
contrat de mise à disposition	contract making someone/something available
contrat de mission	contract for a task
contrat de mission à l'exportation	contract for a project as expatriate

contrat de professionnalisation	type of contract combining work and work training
contrat de projet	a professional category of work used for a particular project, eg for engineers.
contrat de travail à durée déterminée (CDD)	fixed term work contract
contrat de travail à durée déterminée à objet défini	fixed term contract for a specific task
contrat de travail à durée déterminée à terme précis	fixed term contract where the dates are set at the outset
contrat de travail à durée déterminée sans terme précis	fixed term contract where the dates are not set but the determining event is set
contrat de travail à durée déterminée senior	type of *CDD* subject to various formalities, that can be used to employ a person aged over 57 who has been seeking work for more than 3 months
contrat de travail à durée indéterminée (CDI)	work contract without fixed term
contrat de travail à temps partagé	job share contract
contrat de travail à temps partiel	part time contract
contrat de travail intermittent	contract for intermittent work
contrat de travail saisonnier	seasonal work contract
contrat de travail temporaire (l'intérim) (CTT)	temporary work contract
contrats de travail destinés à l'aménagement du temps de travail	contracts intended to assist in organisation of work time
contrats de travail destinés à la formation et/ou à l'insertion	contracts for the purpose of work training/ development or re-integration in employment
contrat étudiant au sein des établissements d'enseignement supérieur	student contract based in higher education establishment

127

contrat initiative-emploi (CIE) (also CAE)	contract where a subsidy is provided to the employer for the job, generally to enable those who are having difficulties finding employment for either social reasons or reasons relating to the area of work – usually retail sector
contrat unique d'insertion (CUI)	contract intended to assist in reintroduction to the workforce
contrepartie pécuniaire	pecuniary counterpart/recompense
convention d'entreprise	all conventions and agreements concluded at the level of the enterprise or at the level of the establishment
convention de branche	refers to collective convention and agreement at branch and inter-branch level, and also professional agreements defining the conditions of employment and work of employees and various guarantees applicable to them
convention de forfait	an agreement between the employer and employee regarding the number of hours, days or weeks worked
convention de reclassement personalisé	a type of procedure that has been offered by the employer to an employee facing dismissal by the employer on economic grounds, intended to assist them in re-qualifying for or finding other work
convocation	formal requirement to come to a meeting
Cour d'appel	Court of Appeal, both civil and criminal jurisdiction
Cour de cassation	the highest court, the final court of appeal
CV – curriculum vitae	curriculum vitae
déclaration unique d'embauche (DUE)	declaration of details of an employment that must be submitted to the *Ursaff*.
décret	Order with either general or individual effect signed either by the Président de la République or by the Premier Ministre
dédit-formation	the sum to be reimbursed by an employee if their employment ends following a training course

défendeur	defendant
défense	defence
Défenseur des droits	Defender of Rights; an institution set up and recognised in the French constitution to oversee rights, to defend people where their rights may have been abused and to assist in enabling all to benefit from their rights
délai de carence	mandatory break between one event and another
délai de prévenance	notification period
délégation unique du personnel (DUP)	single consolidated body representing the employees, fusing the *DP*s with, where they exist, the *CE* and *CHSCT*
délégué du personnel (DP)	employees' representative
délégué suppléant	deputy delegate
délégué syndical	union representative
délégué titulaire	delegate currently holding the post
délit	level of offence which is sufficiently serious that it may incur a penalty of imprisonment
délit d'entrave	offence of impeding the work of the employee
demande	claim
demandeur	plaintiff
démission	handing in notice
démission abusive	incorrect termination of contract by an employee
dénomination sociale	name of the business (particularly registered name)
DIRECCTE (Direction régionale des entreprises, de la concurrence, de la consommation, du travail) et de l'emploi	Regional authority for businesses, competition, consumption, work and employment

directeur régional des entreprises, de la concurrence, de la consummation, du travail et de l'emploi	the regional director of business, competition, consumption, work and employment
dirigeant	leader, manager
dirigeant d'entreprise	company director
discrimination	discrimination
discrimination directe	direct discrimination
discrimination indirecte	indirect discrimination
document unique d'évaluation des risques professionnels	document setting out the health and safety risks and work and measures to deal with them
dommages-intérêts	damages and interest
droit	law, right (as in a right to)
droit constitutionnel	constitutional right
droit conventionnel	law arising from collective agreements and conventions entered into between unions of employees and of employers
droit individuel à la formation (DIF)	personal right to training
droit social	relating to social welfare, particularly in relation to becoming unemployed, retiring, work holidays, incapacity etc and often including employment issues generally
durée effectif/temps de travail effectif	actual working time as defined
durée hebdomadaire maximale	weekly working time limit
durée journalière maximale	daily limit on (working) time
durée légale	legal notional time to be worked in a given period
durée maximale absolue	absolute time limit

durée maximale du travail	maximum working period
durée maximale moyenne	maximum average limit
échelle des sanctions	scale of sanctions
embaucher	to take on in employment
emploi	employment
employeur	employer
enseigne	business sign
entreprise	an "autonomous entity, created and used by one or more people carrying out an economic activity using people and property" (Ass. Plén., 16 mars 1990, D. 1990.305)
entreprise de travail temporaire (ETT)	temporary work enterprise
entretien	meeting/conversation
entretien préalable	initial meeting prior to taking steps being considered
essai professionnel	form of professional assessment carried out prior to any contract being entered into
exclusivité	exclusivity
exécutoire	enforceable
faisceau d'indices	set of criteria
faute disciplinaire	disciplinary fault
faute grave	behaviour sufficiently serious to allow the employer to terminate the contract without notice and without *indemnité* except for *congés payés*
faute légère	the most minor category of offence – dismissal not allowed
faute lourde	behaviour more serious than *faute grave* – also deprives the employee also of the right to payment in lieu of leave

faute sérieuse	the second degree of seriousness of offence – may lead to dismissal where the employee is on a *CDI* because the behaviour is prejudicial to the enterprise
forfait-jours	allocated number of days to be worked
formation professionnelle	professional development/training
GPEC (*Gestion prévisionnelle de l'emploi et des compétences*)	strategic workforce planning
greffe	court clerk
grève	strike
grève de solidarité	strike where the claims do not relate to the striking employees themselves but are in support of the rights of e.g. one other employee
grève perlée	a go-slow or working in a voluntarily defective manner; not considered under French law to be technically a strike as the work continues to occur
grève tournante	where stops affect successive parts of the service of the enterprise
harcèlement moral	bullying
harcèlement sexuel	sexual harassment
Haute autorité de lutte contre les discriminations et pour l'égalité (Halde)	High authority for action against discrimination and for equality
heures complémentaires	additional hours – hours worked by part-time workers in excess of those set in their contract
heures supplémentaires	supplementary hours (worked per allocated period)
homologuer	to formalise
horaire collectif de travail	working time that is uniform for all the employees
horaire individualisé	personal working time

huissier	a type of qualified legal professional who may deal with process-serving, debt recovery and enforcing judgments
inaptitude professionnelle	professional inaptitude
indemnité compensatrice	pay for the employee in lieu of any untaken leave, paid at the end of the contract
indemnité conventionnelle	agreed payment
indemnité de congés payés	holiday pay
indemnité de fin de contrat/ indemnité de précarité	compensation to an employee at the end of a *CDD*
indemnité légale de licenciement	legal payment for dismissal
inspecteur du travail	work inspector employed by the State
insuffisance professionnelle	professional insufficiency
jeune travailleur	young worker, aged at least 15 and under 18 years old
jour chômé	paid day of public holiday
jour férié	bank holiday
jour franc	24 hours, not including the day of the event in question
journée de solidarité	day of solidarity
juge	judge
juge d'instruction	criminal judicial section/person whose job is to gather together all the relevant information and evidence *(les preuves)* and to consider the charges *(les charges)* against the accused *(la personne mise en examen)*
jugement	judgement
jugement d'urgence	urgent judgement
jurisprudence	interpretation made by the courts or *tribunaux* of the texts of the laws and conventions during the course of court proceedings

l'état	the State
l'ouverture des droits	commencement of rights
lettre de candidature	letter (usually) accompanying a CV in support of an application for a (work) position
lettre recommandé avec accusé de réception (LRAR)	signed-for letter with acknowledgment of receipt
licenciement	dismissal
licenciement abusive/ vexatoire	abusive/vexatious dismissal
licenciement économique	dismissal for economic reasons; the French version of redundancy; however, there are differences
licenciement irrégulier	irregular dismissal
licenciement nul	void/voidable dismissal
licenciement pour motif personnel	dismissal for reasons relating to the employee
licenciement sans cause réelle et sérieuse	dismissal for no real or serious cause
licenciement vexatoire/ abusive	vexatious/abusive dismissal
livre de paie	register of salaries, bonuses etc
lock-out	lock-out
loi	a law; a rule written, of general effect and permanent, created by Parlement
maintien leur capacité à occupier leur poste de travail	maintain capability to do a job
maisons de l'emploi	bodies in each region of France, for bringing together the State, the *ANPE*, the *ASSEDIC*, *collectivités territoriales* and, where applicable, consular bodies, *missions locales*
maître d'apprentissage	person to whom an apprentice is apprenticed

majoration de salaire	salary increase
médiation	mediation
micro-entreprise – MIC (très petit entreprise – TPM)	business with fewer than 10 employees in a business year, and a turnover of no more than 2 million euros
mise à pied disciplinaire	suspension
missions locales pour l'insertion professionnelle et sociale des jeunes	local organisations set up to assist young people aged 16-25 with regard to search for work, with training and qualifications, housing and health matters
mobilité géographique	geographical mobility
motif personnel	reason relating to the individual in question, rather than e.g. to the enterprise
mutation	transfer
mutations technologiques	technological changes
négociation annuelle obligatoire (NAO)	mandatory annual pay negotiation
notaire	legal professional similar to a solicitor (but not handling contentious matters)/notary public; have a monopoly on some procedures relating to eg property transactions, and deal with non-contentious matters including property work, company and commercial, tax, succession etc.
nulle	void
obligation réciproque	reciprocal obligation
ordonnance	Act made by the government, with the authorisation of Parlement, with regard to matters of law. Before ratification by Parlement it will have the effect of a réglement; afterwards, it will have the effect of law
Organisme Paritaire Agréé au Titre du Congé Individuel de Formation (Opacif)	Approved Joint Organisation for the Individual Training Leave

135

organismes de prévoyance	bodies providing social security
ouvrier	person working in production
pacs (pacte civil de solidarité)	civil union between two adults
par anticipation	in advance (e.g. taking paid leave before waiting for the end of the reference period)
Parlement	Parliament
participation financière des salariés	financial participation of the employees
partie lesée	injured party
périmètres d'usage de consummation exceptionnel	habitual perimeters of exceptional consumption – urban zones of more than one million inhabitants with typical Sunday purchasing, the importance of the clientele concerned and the distance of them from this perimeter
périod d'essai	trial period
période de référence	reference period – may refer to the applicable year for calculating holiday entitlement
période probatoire	where a current employee enters a trial period to assess them for a new position within the organisation
personne mise en examen	the accused in criminal matters
plaideur	litigant
plan de formation	training plan
plan de sauvegarde de l'emploi	plan to safeguard the employment
petites et moyennes entreprises (PMI)	small and medium sized businesses – fewer than 250 employees and a turnover of less than 50 million euros or a balance sheet over 43 million euros
Pôle emploi	organisation responsible for providing the public service of employment assistance
pont	extra day of public holiday that may be given

	by an employer where a bank holiday does not fall next to the weekly rest day but is one or two days away, to "fill in" the gap
pouvoir d'alerte	power to make an alert/draw matters to attention so that they may be addressed
pouvoir disciplinaire	disciplinary power
pouvoir réglementaire	power to make the rules/regulations
préavis	notice (period)
préfet	person appointed in a given region to be the formal representative of the State
préjudice moral	moral prejudice e.g. hurt feelings, psychological damage, non-physical non-economic loss etc.
préscription des faits fautifs	limitation period for the facts that are at fault
préscription des sanctions disciplinaires	limitation period for sanctions
prétention	claim
preuve	evidence
prime	bonus
principe de non-discrimination	principle of non-discrimination
prise d'acte	termination of a contract by the employee because of failures by the employer; this may equate to a *licenciement* if the legal issues and facts support this, or it may amount to a *démission*
procédure disciplinaire	disciplinary procedure
profession libérale	specific profession requiring certain types of formal training and structure of employment, e.g. lawyers, doctors, architects
proportionnalité	proportionality
recommandé avec accusé de réception	recorded delivery with signed for receipt

137

reconversion	redeployment
réduction de temps de travail (RTT)	reduction of work time
régistre des accidents du travail bénins	register of minor work accidents
régistré des contrôles techniques de sécurité	register of safety inspections
régistre des délégués du personnel	register of the *délégués du personnel* (specific category of personnel representatives)
régistre des mises en demeure	register of letters before action (letter sent requiring action failing which court proceedings may be commenced)
régistre du CHSCT (comité d'hygiène, de sécurité et des conditions de travail)	register of the committee of health, safety
régistre du commerce des sociétés	companies register
régistre unique de personnel	register of employees
règlement	rule created by the competent authorities to have general (rather than individual or limited) effect
règlement intérieur	internal rules/regulations
rémunération forfaitaire	remuneration for the *forfait*
répertoire des métiers	register of non-incorporated businesses
repos compensateur de remplacement	rest hours given to compensate for supplementary hours worked
repos hebdomadaire	weekly rest
repos quotidien	daily rest
réprésentant de la section syndicale	representative of the union section in a business/establishment where the union is not yet sufficiently representative to be eligible for certain matters
requalification-sanction	sanction of re-qualification of a contract
résiliation judiciaire	court order terminating a contract

rétrogradation	demotion
revenu de solidarité active (RSA)	solidarity benefit, to ensure that households have the basic minimum required for human dignity
rupture abusive	abusive termination of contract
rupture anticipé	early termination of the contract i.e. before its term or minimum term or before the accomplishment of its objective(s)
rupture conventionnelle	mutual break of the contract
rupture du contrat du travail	breaking of the employment contract
rupture judiciaire	a termination of the contract obtained by order of the court using a set procedure
rupture unilatérale	unilateral breaking of the contract
salaire	remuneration for employment, salary
salaire de base	basic salary, not including bonuses etc.
salaire journalier de référence	daily salary calculated as an average over a year according to a set calculation
Salaire minimum interprofessionnel de croissance (SMIC)	minimum wage
salarié	employee
sanctions disciplinaires	disciplinary action
se démettre	resign
secret professionel	trade secret
section syndicale	a group amongst the workforce who have been nominated by the union to carry out negotiations etc.
sécurité sociale	the State body in France which handles family, health and retirement benefits and litigation arising
service de santé au travail (SST)	Work health service
service public d'emploi	public employment service

service social du travail	work social service
signifier à	to serve on
société anonyme	type of limited company
sous astreinte	on call
stage	work experience placement
statut	set of law or laws setting out the rights/ obligations of a particular State organisation or set of agents or workers
subvention de fonctionnement	fund to enable to beneficiary to function
syndicat	union
technicien	person with a particular expertise or technical knowledge
temps d'astreinte	time on call
temps de travail effectif/ durée effectif	actual working time as defined
transaction	mutual arrangement dealing with the consequences of a dismissal previously notified, handing in of notice or a court process
transparence	transparency
travail	work
travail dissimulé (clandestin)	illegal work
travailleur intérimaire	temporary worker
Très petit entreprise (TPM) (micro-entreprise MIC)	business with fewer than 10 employees in a business year, and a turnover of no more than 2 million euros
tribunal d' instance (TI)	lower court
tribunal de grande instance (TGI)	upper court
tribunaux de commerce	commercial courts

Ursaff (Unions de Recouvrement des Cotisations de Sécurité Sociale et d'Allocations Familiales)	organisations for the payment of social security and family benefit contributions
valeur ajoutée	value added
visite médicale d'embauche	medical undertaken when starting employment
VRP (Voyageur, représentant et placier)	a French term for a class of salaried sales representatives

English	French
absolute time limit	*durée maximale absolue*
abusive termination of contract	*rupture abusive*
abusive/vexatious dismissal	*licenciement abusive/vexatoire*
accused in criminal matters	*personne mise en examen*
Act made by the government, with the authorisation of *Parlement*, with regard to matters of law. Before ratification by *Parlement* it will have the effect of a *réglement*; afterwards, it will have the effect of law	*ordonnance*
actual working time as defined	*durée effectif/temps de travail effectif*
actual working time as defined	*temps de travail effectif /durée effectif*
additional hours – hours worked by part-time workers in excess of those set in their contract	*heures complémentaires*
adoption leave	*congé adoption*
agencies (local) set up to assist young people aged 16-25 with regard to search for work, with training and qualifications, housing and health matters	*missions locales pour l'insertion professionnelle et sociale des jeunes*
agreed payment	*indemnité conventionnelle*

141

agreement (e.g. for dealing with the consequences of a dismissal previously notified, handing in of notice or a court process)	*transaction*
agreement between one or more of the employers and one or more of the representatives of the employees (usually unions) in a given sector of work	*accord de branche*
agreement between the employer and the representatives of the employees/union there	*accord d'entreprise*
agreement of wishes with a view to achieve a legal effect sought by the parties to the agreement	*accord*
agricultural mutual	*caisse de mutualité agricole*
annual pay négociation that is mandatory	*négociation annuelle obligatoire (NAO)*
apprenticeship contract	*contrat d'apprentissage*
apprenticeships (specific types of work placements specifically to lead to particular types of qualification i.e. in particular professional or technological diplomas of the second level or superior or a type of professional qualification)	*apprentissage*
Approved Joint Organisation for the Individual Training Leave	*Organisme Paritaire Agréé au Titre du Congé Individuel de Formation (Opacif)*
assessment of work carried out prior to any contract being entered into	*essai professionnel*
Association (national) for assistance for foreigners and migrants	*ANAEM (l'Agence national de l'accueil des étrangers et des migrants)*
Association (national) for training of adults	*AFPA (l'Association nationale pour la formation professionnelle des adultes)*
Association for Employment in Industry and Trade (former body –	*ASSEDIC (Association pour l'emploi dans l'industrie et le commerce)*

now merged with the *ANPE* into the *Pôle emploi*)

authority (regional) for businesses, competition, consumption, work and employment	*DIRECCTE (Direction régionale des entreprises, de la concurrence, de la consommation, du travail et de l'emploi)*
bank holiday	*jour férié*
behaviour more serious than *faute grave* – also deprives the employee also of the right to payment in lieu of leave	*faute lourde*
benefit to ensure that households have the basic minimum income required for human dignity	*revenu de solidarité active (RSA)*
bereavement holiday entitlement for a death	*congé de solidarité familiale*
bodies in each region of France, for bringing together the State, the *ANPE*, the *ASSEDIC*, *collectivités territoriales* and, where applicable, consular bodies, *missions locales*	*maisons de l'emploi*
bonus	*prime*
break between one event and another	*délai de carence*
break of the contract by agreement	*rupture conventionnelle*
breaking of the contract unilaterally	*rupture unilatérale*
breaking of the employment contract	*rupture du contrat du travail*
bullying	*harcèlement moral*
burden of proof	*charge de la preuve*
business sign	*enseigne*
central enterprise committee for the group, where a business comprises several establishments	*comité centrale d'entreprise*

Civil code	*Code civil*
civil court section	*chambre civile*
civil union between two adults	*pacs (pacte civil de solidarité)*
claim	*demande, prétention*
classification of the employee in a deemed level or category of work	*classement*
code for the principal activity from a set list of codes	*code APE (Activité Principale Exercée)*
Code of Commerce	*Code de commerce*
Code of Employment Law	*Code de travail*
collective conflict	*conflit collectif*
collective convention and agreement at branch and inter-branch level, and also professional agreements defining the conditions of employment and work of employees and various guarantees applicable to them	*convention de branche*
commencement of rights	*l'ouverture des droits*
commercial court section	*chambre commerciale*
commercial courts (e.g. price disputes)	*tribunaux de commerce*
commission that is regional joint inter-professional commission – composed of representatives from both employees' unions and employers' groups, to advise and assist employees of and employers of businesses with fewer than 11 employees	*commission paritaire régionale interprofessionnelle*
committee for hygiene and safety and work conditions	*comité d'hygiène, de sécurité et des conditions de travail (CHSCT)*
committee for the enterprise for each establishment in a business comprising several establishments	*comité d'établissement*
companies register	*régistre du commerce des sociétés*

company, type of limited	*société anonyme*
company director	*dirigeant d'entreprise*
compensation to an employee at the end of a *CDD*	*indemnité de fin de contrat/ indemnité de précarité*
competition	*concurrence*
comprising more than one judge/ magistrate etc.	*collégiale*
Conseil d'État "advises the Government on the preparation of bills, ordinances and certain decrees. It also answers the Government's queries on legal affairs and conducts studies upon the request of the Government or through its own initiative regarding administrative or public policy issues. *Conseil d'État* is the highest administrative jurisdiction – it is the final arbiter of cases relating to executive power, local authorities, independent public authorities, public administration agencies or any other agency invested with public authority." http://www.conseil-etat.fr/en/	*Conseil d'Etat*
Constitution	*Constitution*
constitutional right	*droit constitutionnel*
constructive dismissal – closest equivalent: termination of a contract by the employee because of failures by the employer; this may equate to a *licenciement* if the legal issues and facts support this, or it may amount to a *démission*	*prise d'acte*
contract	*contrat*
contract for intermittent work	*contrat de travail intermittent*
contract for professional qualification	*contrat de professionalisation*

contract for project or job of work – previously mainly for construction industry but now for general use as well	*contrat de chantier ou d'opération*
contract for task	*contrat de mission*
contract for temporary work	*contrat de travail temporaire (CTT)*
contract intended to assist in reintroduction to the workforce	*contrat unique d'insertion (CUI)*
contract making someone/something available	*contrat de mise à disposition*
contract type combining work and work training	*contrat de professionnalisation*
contract type particularly aimed at helping young people having various types of difficulty obtaining work, involving subsidy to the employer and additional support for the employee by e.g. tutors in the business and assistance from State bodies	*contrat d'avenir (CA)*
contract where a subsidy is provided to the employer for the job, generally to enable those who are having difficulties finding employment for either social reasons or reasons relating to the area of work – usually retail sector	*contrat d'accompagnement dans l'emploi (CAE)* (also *CIE*)
contract where a subsidy is provided to the employer for the job, generally to enable those who are having difficulties finding employemnt for either social reasons or reasons relating to the area of work – usually retail sector	*contrat initiative-emploi (CIE)* (also *CAE*)
contracts for the purpose of work training/development or re-integration in employment	*contrats de travail destinés à la formation et/ou à l'insertion*
contracts intended to assist in organisation of work time	*contrats de travail destinés à l'aménagement du temps de travail*

146

conventions and agreements concluded at the level of the enterprise or at the level of the establishment	*convention d'entreprise*
court clerk	*greffe*
Court of Appeal *(Cour d'appel)* section dealing with appeals related to the jurisdictional aspects of criminal matters	*chambre d'accusation*
Court of Appeal, both civil and criminal jurisdiction	*Cour d'appel*
court order terminating a contract	*résiliation judiciaire*
criminal charge/accusation	*charge*
criminal court section	*chambre correctionnelle*
criminal judicial section/person whose job is to gather together all the relevant information and evidence *(les preuves)* and to consider the charges *(les charges)* against the accused *(la personne mise en examen)*	*juge d'instruction*
criteria (set of)	*faisceau d'indices*
curriculum vitae	*CV – curriculum vitae*
daily limit on (working) time	*durée journalière maximale*
daily rest	*repos quotidien*
daily salary calculated as an average over a year according to a set calculation	*salaire journalier de référence*
damages and interest	*dommages-intérêts*
day of 24 hours, not including the day of the event in question	*jour franc*
day of solidarity	*journée de solidarité*
days allocated to be worked	*forfait-jours*
dealing with so-called social matters *(droit social)*	*chambre sociale*

declaration of details of an employment that must be submitted to the *Ursaff*	*déclaration unique d'embauche (DUE)*
defence	*défense*
defendant	*défendeur*
Defender of Rights, an institution set up and recognised in the French constitution to oversee rights, to defend people where their rights may have been abused and to assist in enabling all to benefit from their rights	*Défenseur des droits*
delegate currently holding the post	*délégué titulaire*
demotion	*rétrogradation*
deputy delegate	*délégué suppléant*
direct discrimination	*discrimination directe*
disciplinary action	*sanctions disciplinaires*
disciplinary fault	*faute disciplinaire*
disciplinary panel	*conseil de discipline*
disciplinary power	*pouvoir disciplinaire*
disciplinary procedure	*procédure disciplinaire*
discrimination	*discrimination*
dismissal	*licenciement*
dismissal for economic reasons	*licenciement économique*
dismissal for no real or serious cause	*licenciement sans cause réelle et sérieuse*
dismissal for reasons relating to the employee	*licenciement pour motif personnel*
document or action leading to a legal effect	*acte*
early termination of the contract i.e. before its term or minimum term or before the accomplishment of its objective(s)	*rupture anticipé*

effective working time as defined, plus breaks, meal times, interruptions	*amplitude journalière*
employ (take on in employment)	*embaucher*
employee	*salarié*
employee category of those receiving over a certain minimum salary, or having a certain level of professional qualification	*cadre*
employees representative body – single consolidated body representing the employees, fusing the *DP*s with, where they exist, the *CE* and *CHSCT*	*délégation unique du personnel (DUP)*
employees' representative	*délégué du personnel (DP)*
employer	*employeur*
employment	*emploi*
enforcable	*exécutoire*
enterprise (specifically, an "autonomous entity, created and used by one or more people carrying out an economic activity using people and property" (Ass. Plén., 16 mars 1990, D. 1990.305)	*entreprise*
evidence	*preuve*
exclusivity	*exclusivité*
expatriat contract	*contrat de mission à l'exportation*
extra day of public holiday that may be given by an employer where a bank holiday does not fall next to the weekly rest day but is one or two days away, to "fill in" the gap	*pont*
financial participation of the employees	*participation financière des salariés*
fixed term contract for a specific task	*CDD à objet défini*

fixed term contract for older employees	*CDD senior*
fixed term contract where the dates are not set but the determining event is set	*CDD sans terme précis*
fixed term contract where the dates are set at the outset	*CDD à term précis*
fixed term work contract	*contrat de travail à durée déterminée (CDD)*
formal requirement to come to a meeting	*convocation*
formalise	*homologuer*
fund to enable to beneficiary to function	*subvention de fonctionnement*
geographical mobility	*mobilité géographique*
giving in notice	*démission*
go-slow or working in a voluntarily defective manner; not considered under French law to be technically a strike as the work continues to occur	*grève perlée*
guarantee of employment clause	*clause de garantie d'emploi*
habitual perimeters of exceptional consumption – urban zones of more than un million inhabitants with typical Sunday purchasing, the importance of the clientele concerned and the distance of them from this perimeter	*périmetres d'usage de consummation exceptionnel*
health and safety risks document also including work and measures to deal with them	*document unique d'évaluation des risques professionnels*
health service at work	*service de santé au travail (SST)*
High authority for action against discrimination and for equality	*Haute autorité de lutte contre les discriminations et pour l'égalité (Halde)*
highest court, the final court of appeal	*Cour de cassation*

holiday account	*compte épargne-temps (CET)*
holiday for a sick child	*congé pour un enfant malade*
holiday pay	*indemnité de congés payés*
holiday related to the birth or adoption of a child	*congé lié à la naissance ou à l'adoption d'un enfant*
holiday related to the death of a father, mother, brother, sister, father-in-law or mother-in-law of the employee	*congé lié au décès du père, de la mere, d'un frère, d'une soeur, du beau-père, de la belle-mère du salarié*
holiday related to the marriage of a child	*congé lié à la naissance ou à l'adoption d'un enfant*
holiday related to the marriage of the employee	*congé lié au mariage du salarié*
holiday to set up a business	*congé pour création d'entreprise*
holiday/leave	*congés*
hours agreement between the employer and employee regarding the number of hours, days or weeks worked	*convention de forfait*
illegal work	*travail dissimulé (clandestin)*
in advance (eg taking paid leave before waiting for the end of the reference period)	*par anticipation*
incorrect termination of contract by an employee	*démission abusive*
indirect discrimination	*discrimination indirecte*
initial meeting prior to taking steps being considered	*entretien préalable*
injured party	*partie lesée*
internal rules/regulations	*règlement intérieur*
interpretation made by the courts or *tribunaux* of the texts of the laws and conventions during the course of court proceedings	*jurisprudence*

irregular dismissal	*licenciement irrégulier*
job share contract	*contrat de travail à temps partagé*
judge	*juge*
judgment	*jugement*
law arising from collective agreements and conventions entered into between unions of employees and of employers	*droit conventionnel*
law or laws setting out the rights/ obligations of a particular State organisation or set of agents or workers	*statut*
law, right (as in a right to...)	*droit*
law; a rule written, of general effect and permanent, created by Parlement	*loi*
lawyer qualified as French lawyer in France, professional qualification similar to solicitor, including advocacy but not covering all the same aspects of the legal profession, some of which are carried outfor example by notaires, who have an entirely separate qualification	*avocat*
leader, manager	*dirigeant*
leave for training (for an individual)	*congé individuel de formation (CIF)*
legal notional time to be worked in a given period	*durée légale*
legal professional similar to a solicitor (but not handling contentious matters)/notary public; have a monopoly on some procedures relating to eg property transactions, and deal with non-contentious matters including property work, company and commercial, tax, succession etc.	*notaire*
length of employment	*ancienneté*
letter (usually) accompanying a CV in support of an application for a (work) position	*lettre de candidature*

limitation period for sanctions	*préscription des sanctions disciplinaires*
limitation period for the facts that are at fault	*préscription des faits fautifs*
litigant	*plaideur*
lock-out	*lock-out*
lower court	*tribunal d'instance (TI)*
lowest local administrative division in France	*commune*
main holiday	*congé principal*
maintain capability to do a job	*maintien leur capacité à occupier leur poste de travail*
maternity leave	*congé de maternité*
maternity leave after the birth	*congé postnatal*
maternity leave prior to the birth	*congé prénatal*
maximum average limit	*durée maximale moyenne*
maximum working period	*durée maximale du travail*
mediation	*médiation*
medical taken on commencing employment	*visite médicale d'embauche*
meeting/conversation	*entretien*
minimum wage	*SMIC (Salaire minimum interprofessionnel de croissance)*
minor offence – dismissal not allowed	*faute légère*
mobility time off, to help employees return to stable work by seeking assistance, training and work. Applies to businesses with at least 100 employees and who have reached an *accord collectif* about plans to manage the jobs and the skills	*congé de mobilité*

moral prejudice e.g. hurt feelings, psychological damage, non-physical non-economic loss etc.	*préjudice moral*
name of the business (particularly registered name)	*dénomination sociale*
National work agency – former body now merged with the *ASSEDIC* into the *Pôle emploi*	*ANPE (l'Agence nationale pour l'emploi)*
non-discrimination principle	*principe de non-discrimination*
notice (period)	*préavis*
notification period	*délai de prévenance*
object clause	*clause d'objectifs*
offence of impeding the work of the employee	*délit d'entrave*
offence which is sufficiently serious that it may incur a penalty of imprisonment	*délit*
on call	*sous astreinte*
on-call time	*temps d'astreinte*
order with either general or individual effect signed either by the Président de la République or by the Premier Ministre	*décret*
organisation responsible for providing the public service of employment assistance	*Pôle emploi*
overseer work category set out in conventions collectives. Their role will be to direct, coordinate, or control the work of a certain number of *ouvriers*. There is not a precise legal definition	*agent de maitrise*
paid holiday	*congé payé*
parental education leave	*congé parental d'education*

Parliament	*Parlement*
part time contract	*contrat de travail à temps partiel*
paternity leave	*congé de paternité*
pay for the employee in lieu of any untaken leave, paid at the end of the contract	*indemnité compensatrice*
payment for dismissal	*indemnité légale de licenciement*
pecuniary counterpart/recompense	*contrepartie pécuniaire*
Penal Code	*Code pénal*
pension scheme supplementary to the State one	*caisse de retraite complémentaire*
person to whom an apprentice is apprenticed	*maître d'apprentissage*
plaintiff	*demandeur*
plan to safeguard the employment	*plan de sauvegarde de l'emploi*
power to make an alert/draw matters to attention so that they may be addressed	*pouvoir d'alerte*
power to make the rules/regulations	*pouvoir réglementaire*
process-server also doing debt recovery and enforcing judgments – qualified legal professional	*huissier*
production worker (person working in production)	*ouvrier*
profession requiring certain types of formal training and structure of employment, e.g. lawyers, doctors, architects	*profession libérale*
professional category of work used for a particular project, e.g. for engineers	*contrat de projet*
professional development/training	*formation professionnelle*

professional inaptitude	*inaptitude professionnelle*
professional insufficiency	*insuffisance professionnelle*
proportionality	*proportionnalité*
provisional collective accord for the management of employment and competences	*accord collectif de gestion prévisionnelle des emplois et des compétences*
public bodies that are separate from the State and have legal autonomy and own and manage their own resources	*collectivités territoriales*
public employment service	*service public d'emploi*
public holiday that is paid	*jour chômé*
real and serious cause	*cause réelle et sérieuse*
reason relating to the individual in question, rather than e.g. to the enterprise	*motif personnel*
reciprocal obligation	*obligation réciproque*
record of charitable/voluntary work	*compte d'engagement citoyen*
recorded delivery with signed for receipt	*recommandé avec accusé de réception*
redeployment	*reconversion*
reduction of work time	*réduction de temps de travail (RTT)*
redundancy	*licenciement économique* is the closest French equivalent, but there are various differences
reference period – may refer to the applicable year for calculating holiday entitlement	*période de référence*
regional director of business, competition, consumption, work and employment	*directeur régional des entreprises, de la concurrence, de la consommation, du travail et de l'emploi*
register of délégués du personnel	*régistre des délégués du personnel*

register of employees	*régistre unique de personnel*
register of letters before action	*régistre des mises en demeure*
register of minor work accidents	*régistre des accidents du travail bénins*
register of non-incorporated businesses	*répertoire des métiers*
register of safety inspections	*régistre des contrôles techniques de sécurité*
register of salaries, bonuses etc.	*livre de paie*
register of the *CHSCT*	*régistre du CHSCT*
remuneration for employment, salary	*salaire*
remuneration for the *forfait*	*rémunération forfaitaire*
repeated behaviour	*agissements répétés*
representative of the State appointed in a given region	*préfet*
representative of the union section in a business/establishment where the union is not yet sufficiently representative to be eligible for certain matters	*réprésentant de la section syndicale*
reprimand, usually in the form of a written warning and tending to be serious including a final warning	*blâme*
requalification assistance procedure that has been offered by the employer to an employee facing dismissal by the employer on economic grounds, intended to assist them in re-qualifying for or finding other work	*convention de reclassement personalisé*
residence permit (10-year duration)	*carte de résident*
resign	*se démettre*
rest hours give to compensate for supplementary hours worked	*repos compensateur de remplacement*

rule created by the competent authorities to have general (rather than individual or limited) effect	*règlement*
sabbatical	*congé sabbatique*
salaried sales representatives – specific work grouping	*VRP (Voyageur, représentant et placier)*
salary – basic, not including bonuses etc.	*salaire de base*
salary increase	*majoration de salaire*
sanction of re-qualification of a contract	*requalification-sanction*
sanctions scale	*échelle des sanctions*
seasonal work contract	*contrat de travail saisonnier*
second degree of offence – may lead to dismissal where the employee is on a *CDI* because the behaviour is prejudicial to the enterprise	*faute sérieuse*
senior person *CDD – CDD* type subject to various formalities, that can be used to employ a person aged over 57 who has been seeking work for more than 3 months	*CDD senior*
serious fault behaviour: sufficiently serious to allow the employer to terminate the contract without notice and without *indemnité* except for *congés payés*	*faute grave*
serve on	*signifier à*
sexual harassment	*harcèlement sexuel*
share (particular type)	*certificat d'investissement*
short-term residence permit	*carte de séjour temporaire*
signed-for letter with acknowledgment of receipt	*lettre recommandé avec accusé de réception (LRAR)*

small and medium-sized businesses – fewer than 250 employees and a turnover of less than 50 million euros or a balance sheet over 43 million euros	*petites et moyennes entreprises (PMI)*
small business, one with fewer than 10 employees in a business year, and a turnover of no more than 2 million euros	*micro-entreprise – MIC (très petit entreprise – TPM)*
social security and family benefit contributions organisations	*Ursaff (Unions de Recouvrement des Cotisations de Sécurité Sociale et d'Allocations Familiales)*
social security bodies providing social security	*organismes de prévoyance*
social security State body in France which handles family, health and retirement benefits and litigation arising	*sécurité sociale*
social service at work	*service social du travail*
social welfare law, particularly in relation to becoming unemployed, retiring, work holidays, incapacity etc. and often including employment issues generally	*droit social*
strategic workforce planning	*GPEC – (Gestion prévisionnelle de l'emploi et des compétences)*
strike	*grève*
strike where the claims do not relate to the striking employees themselves but are in support of the rights of e.g. one other employee	*grève de solidarité*
student contract based in higher education establishment	*contrat étudiant au sein des établissements d'enseignement supérieur*
suitability of employee to job	*adaptation des salaries à leur poste de travail*
sum to be reimbursed by an employee if their employment ends following a training course	*dédit-formation*

supplementary hours (worked per allocated period)	*heures supplémentaires*
suspension	*mise à pied disciplinaire*
technical knowledge or similar particular expertise person	*technicien*
technological changes	*mutations technologiques*
temporary work contract	*contrat de travail temporaire (l'intérim)*
temporary work enterprise	*entreprise de travail temporaire (ETT)*
temporary worker	*travailleur intérimaire*
termination of the contract obtained by order of the court using a set procedure	*rupture judiciaire*
the State	*l'état*
time off for training, to take steps to seek other work etc.; applicable in businesses of at least 1,000 employees	*congé de reclassement*
total supplementary hours over a year	*contingent annuel d'heures supplémentaires*
trade secret	*secret professionel*
training centre for apprentices	*centre de formation des apprentis (CFA)*
training personal entitlement	*droit individuel à la formation (DIF)*
training plan	*plan de formation*
transfer	*mutation*
transparency	*transparence*
trial period	*période d'essai*
trial period to assess for a new position within the organisation	*période probatoire*

unemployment benefit	*allocations chômage*
unemployment benefit – can also refer to unemployment insurance	*assurance chômage*
union	*syndicat*
union nominated group amongst the workforce who carry out negotiations etc.	*section syndicale*
union representative	*délégué syndical*
upper court	*tribunal de grande instance (TGI)*
urgent judgment	*jugement d'urgence*
use for a particular purpose	*affection*
value added	*valeur ajoutée*
vexatious/abusive dismissal	*licenciement vexatoire/abusive*
void	*nulle*
void/voidable dismissal	*licenciement nul*
wage slip	*bulletin de salaire*
warning	*avertissment*
weekly rest	*repos hebdomadaire*
weekly working time limit	*durée hebdomadaire maximale*
work	*travail*
work contract without fixed term	*contrat de travail à durée indéterminée (CDI)*
work experience placement	*stage*
work inspector employed by the State	*inspecteur du travail*
work stops affecting successive parts of the service of the enterprise	*grève tournante*
working time set for an individual	*horaire individualisé*

working time that is uniform for all the employees	*horaire collectif de travail*
works council	*comité d'entreprise (CE)*
writ, summons	*assignation*
young worker, aged at least 15 and under 18 years	*jeune travailleur*

Index

Lightning Source UK Ltd.
Milton Keynes UK
UKHW011827061118
331882UK00002B/13/P